GET RESULTS!

Dictionary of
Grammar

Dictionary of
Grammar

GEDDES & GROSSET

© 1998 Geddes & Grosset Ltd

This edition published 1998 by Geddes & Grosset Ltd,
David Dale House, New Lanark

ISBN 1 85534 364 9

Printed and bound in UK

2 4 6 8 10 9 7 5 3 1

A

a *see* **indefinite article**.

a-, an-
A prefix derived from Greek, meaning 'not', 'without'. Older words using it include agnostic, anarchy, anonymous. Several modern words have been formed using it, as in apolitical, asexual, atypical.

abbreviation
A shortened form of words, usually used as a space-saving technique and becoming increasingly common in modern usage. Abbreviations cause problems with regard to punctuation. The common question asked is whether the letters of an abbreviation should be separated by full stops. In modern usage the tendency is to omit full stops from abbreviations. This is most true of abbreviations involving initial capital letters, as in TUC, BBC, EC and USA. In such cases full stops should definitely not be used if one or some of the initial letters do not belong to a full word. Thus 'television' is abbreviated to TV and 'educationally subnormal' to ESN.

There are usually no full stops in abbreviations involving the first and last letters of a word (contractions)—Dr, Mr, Rd, St—but this is a matter of taste.

An abbreviation involving the first few letters of a word, as in

'Prof' (Professor), is the most likely to a have full stop, as in 'Feb.' (February), but again this is now a matter of taste.

Plurals of abbreviations are mostly formed by adding lower-case *s*, as in Drs, JPs, TVs. Note the absence of apostrophes.

See also ACRONYMS.

ablative
A case in Latin grammar that expressed 'by, with or from'. In English this case does not exist, prepositional phrases being used its place.

-able
A suffix meaning 'that can be', as in laughable, readable, wash-able. See ADJECTIVE.

abstract noun
A noun which is the name of a thing that cannot be touched but refers to a quality, concept or idea. Examples of abstract nouns include 'anger', 'beauty', 'courage', 'Christianity', 'dan-ger', 'fear', 'greed', 'hospitality', 'ignorance', 'jealousy', 'kudos', 'loyalty', 'Marxism', 'need', 'obstinacy', 'pain', 'quality', 'resist-ance', 'safety', 'truth', 'unworthiness', 'vanity', 'wisdom', 'xeno-phobia', 'youth', 'zeal'. See *also* CONCRETE NOUN.

accent
(1) A regional or individual way of speaking or pronouncing words, as in 'a Glasgow accent'.

(2) A word meaning 'emphasis', as in 'In hotel the accent is on the second syllable of the word' or 'In fashion this year the ac-cent is on longer skirts'.

(3) Any of certain symbols used on some foreign words

adopted into English. In modern usage, which has a tendency to punctuate less than formerly was the case, accents are frequently omitted. For example, an actor's part in a play is now usually spelt 'role' but originally it was spelt 'rôle', the accent on o being called a circumflex. The accent is most likely to be retained if it affects the pronunciation. Thus 'cliché' and 'divorcé' usually retain the acute accent, as it is called, on the e. On the other hand, the accent known as the cedilla is frequently omitted from beneath the c in words such as 'façade/facade', although it is there to indicate that the c is soft, pronounced like an s, rather than a hard sound, pronounced like a k. The grave accent is retained in English in some words and phrases derived from French, as *mise en scène*.

accusative
A case in Latin grammar, the equivalent of OBJECTIVE. It is sometimes used in English instead of objective.

acronym
A word that, like some ABBREVIATIONS, is formed from the initial letters of several words. Unlike abbreviations, however, acronyms are pronounced as words rather than as just a series of letters. For example, OPEC (Organization of Petroleum Producing Countries) is pronounced *o-pek* and is thus an acronym, unlike USA (United States of America) which is pronounced as a series of letters and not as a word (*oo-sa* or *yoo-sa*) and is thus an abbreviation.

Acronyms are written without full stops, as in UNESCO (United Nations Educational, Scientific and Cultural Organization). Mostly acronyms are written in capital letters, as in

NASA (National Aeronautics and Space Administration). However, very common acronyms, such as Aids (Acquired Immune Deficiency Syndrome), are written with just an initial capital, the rest of the letters being lower case.

Acronyms that refer to a piece of scientific or technical equipment are written like ordinary words in lower-case letters, as laser (light amplification by simulated emission of radiation.

active voice
One of the two voices that verbs are divided into, the other being PASSIVE VOICE. In verbs in the active voice, commonly called **active verbs**, the subject of the verb performs the action described by the verb. Thus, in the sentence 'The boy threw the ball', 'throw' is in the active voice since the subject of the verb (the boy) is doing the throwing. Similarly, in the sentence 'Her mother was driving the car', 'driving' is in the active voice since it is the subject of the sentence (her mother) that is doing the driving. Similarly, in the sentence 'We saw the cows in the field', 'saw' is the active voice since it is the subject of the sentence (we) that is doing the seeing.

acute accent
A mark placed over some letters in certain languages, such as French, to indicate vowel length, vowel quality, pronunciation, etc. It is found in English in some words that have been borrowed from the French, as in 'fiancé' and 'divorcé', to indicate pronunciation.

-ade
A suffix meaning 'fruit drink', as in lemonade.

adjectival clause

A kind of SUBORDINATE CLAUSE that describes or modifies a noun or pronoun. It is better known by the name RELATIVE CLAUSE.

adjective

A word that describes or gives information about a noun or pronoun. It is said to qualify a noun or pronoun since it limits the word it describes in some way, by making it more specific. Thus, adding the adjective 'red' to 'book' limits 'book', since it means we can forget about books of any other colour. Similarly, adding 'large' to 'book' limits it, since it means we can forget about books of any other size.

Adjectives tell us something about the colour, size, number, quality or classification of a noun or pronoun, as in 'purple curtains', 'jet-black hair', 'bluish eyes'; 'tiny baby', 'large houses', 'biggish gardens', 'massive estates'; five children', 'twenty questions', 'seventy-five books'; 'sad people', 'joyful occasions', 'delicious food', 'civil engineering', 'nuclear physics', 'modern languages', 'Elizabethan drama'.

Several adjectives may modify one noun or pronoun, as in 'the small, black cat', 'an enormous, red-brick, Victorian house'. The order in which they appear is flexible and can vary according to the emphasis one wishes to place on the various adjectives. However, a common sequence is size, quality, colour and classification, as in 'a small, beautiful, pink wild rose' and 'a large, ugly, grey office building'.

Adjectives do not change their form. They remain the same whether the noun to which they refer is singular or plural, or masculine or feminine.

All the above examples of adjectives come before the noun,

but not all adjectives do so. For information on the position of adjectives see ATTRIBUTIVE ADJECTIVE, PREDICATIVE ADJECTIVE, POST-MODIFIER.

Many adjectives are formed from either the past participles of verbs, and so end in -*ed*, or from the present participles and so end in -*ing*. Examples of adjectives ending in -*ed* include 'annoyed', 'blackened', 'coloured', 'damaged', 'escaped', 'fallen', 'guarded', 'heated', 'identified', 'jailed', 'knotted', 'labelled', 'mixed', 'numbered', 'opened', 'pleated', 'recorded', 'satisfied', 'taped', 'used', 'varied', 'walled', 'zoned'. Examples of adjectives ending in -*ing* include 'amusing', 'boring', 'captivating', 'demanding', 'enchanting', 'fading', 'grating', 'horrifying', 'identifying', 'jarring', 'kneeling', 'labouring', 'manufacturing', 'nursing', 'operating', 'parting', 'quivering', 'racing', 'satisfying', 'telling', 'undermining', 'worrying', 'yielding'.

Several adjectives end in -*ical* and are formed by adding -*al* to certain nouns ending in -*ic*. Examples include 'arithmetical', 'comical', 'critical', 'cynical', 'fanatical', 'logical', 'magical', 'musical', 'mystical' and 'sceptical'. Sometimes the adjectives ending in -*ical* are formed from nouns that end in -*ics*. These include 'acoustical', 'ethical', 'hysterical', 'statistical' and 'tropical'. Several adjectives end in -*ic* and are formed from nouns ending in -*ics*. These include 'acoustic', 'acrobatic', 'aerobic', 'athletic', 'economic', 'electronic', 'genetic', 'gymnastic', 'histrionic' and 'linguistic'.

Other common adjectival endings include -*ful*, as in 'beautiful', 'dreadful', 'eventful', 'graceful', 'hateful', 'tearful' and 'youthful'. They also include -*less*, as in 'clueless', 'graceless', 'hatless', 'meaningless' and 'sunless'.

Many adjectives end in -*able* and many end in -*ible*. There are often spelling problems with such adjectives. The following adjectives are likely to be misspelt:

Some adjectives ending in *-able*:

abominable	disreputable	nameable
acceptable	durable	non-flammable
adaptable	durable	objectionable
adorable	enviable	operable
advisable	excitable	palpable
agreeable	excusable	pleasurable
amiable	expendable	preferable
approachable	foreseeable	readable
available	forgettable	recognizable
bearable	forgivable	regrettable
bearable	healable	renewable
beatable	hearable	reputable
believable	immovable	sizeable
blameable	impassable	stoppable
calculable	impeccable	tenable
capable	implacable	tolerable
changeable	impracticable	transferable
comfortable	impressionable	understandable
commendable	indescribable	unmistakable
conceivable	indispensable	usable
definable	inimitable	variable
delectable	insufferable	viable
demonstrable	lamentable	washable
dependable	manageable	wearable
desirable	measurable	winnable
discreditable	memorable	workable

Some adjectives ending in *-ible*:

accessible
admissible
audible
collapsible
combustible
compatible
comprehensible
contemptible
credible
defensible
destructible
digestible
discernible

divisible
edible
exhaustible
expressible
fallible
feasible
flexible
forcible
gullible
indelible
intelligible
irascible
negligible

perceptible
permissible
possible
repressible
reproducible
resistible
responsible
reversible
risible
sensible
susceptible
tangible
visible

See also COMPARISON OF ADJECTIVES, COMPOUNDS, DEMONSTRATIVE DETERMINERS, DETERMINER, FIRST PERSON, INTERROGATIVE ADJECTIVE, SECOND PERSON and THIRD PERSON.

adverb

A word that adds to our information about a VERB, as in 'work rapidly'; about an ADJECTIVE, as in 'an extremely beautiful young woman'; or about another adverb, as in 'sleeping very soundly'. Adverbs are said to modify the words to which they apply since they limit the words in some way and make them more specific. Thus, adding 'slowly' to 'walk', as in 'They walked slowly down the hill', limits the verb 'walk' since all other forms of 'walk', such as 'quickly', 'lazily', etc, have been discarded.

There are several different kinds of adverbs, categorized according to the information they provide about the word they modify. They include adverbs of time, adverbs of place, adverbs of manner, adverbs of degree, adverbs of frequency, adverbs of probability, adverbs of duration and interrogative adverbs.

An **adverb of time** tells us when something happened, and they include such words as 'now', 'then', 'later', 'soon', 'afterwards', 'yesterday', etc, as in 'He is due to arrive now', 'I will call you later', 'She had a rest and went out afterwards', 'They left yesterday'.

An **adverb of place** tells us where something happened. Adverbs of place include such words as 'there', 'here', 'somewhere', 'anywhere', 'thereabouts', 'abroad', 'outdoors', 'overhead', 'underground', 'hither and thither', etc, as in 'I haven't been there', 'They couldn't see her anywhere', 'His family live abroad', and 'We heard a noise overhead'.

An **adverb of manner** tells us how something happens, and they include a wide range of possibilities. Frequently adverbs in this category are formed by adding -ly to an adjective. Examples of these include:

adjective	adverb	adjective	adverb
anxious	anxiously	mean	meanly
bad	badly	narrow	narrowly
cautious	cautiously	pale	palely
dumb	dumbly	quick	quickly
elegant	elegantly	soothing	soothingly
fashionable	fashionably	sound	soundly
fearless	fearlessly	tough	toughly
hot	hotly	unwilling	unwillingly
interested	interestedly	vain	vainly
joking	jokingly	weak	weakly
lame	lamely		

Some adjectives have to be modified in some way before the suffix -*ly* is added to form the adverbs. For example, in adjectives ending in -*y*, the *y* changes to *i* before -*ly* is added. Examples of these include:

adjective	*adverb*	*adjective*	*adverb*
angry	angrily	happy	happily
busy	busily	merry	merrily
canny	cannily	pretty	prettily
dry	drily	silly	sillily
easy	easily	tatty	tattily
funny	funnily	weary	wearily

Note the exceptions 'shyly', 'slyly', 'wryly'.

Adjectives ending in -e frequently drop the e before adding -*ly*. Examples of these include:

adjective	*adverb*	*adjective*	*adverb*
able	ably	peaceable	peaceably
feeble	feebly	true	truly
gentle	gently	unintelligible	unintelligibly

Suffixes other than -*ly* that may be added to adjectives to form adverbs of manner include -*wards*, as in backwards, heavenwards; -*ways*, as in edgeways, sideways; -*wise*, as in clockwise, moneywise.

Some adverbs of manner may take the same form as the adjectives to which they correspond. These include 'fast', 'hard', 'solo', 'straight', 'wrong', as in 'She took the wrong book' and 'Don't get me wrong'.

An **adverb of degree** tells us the degree, extent or intensity of something that happens, and they include 'hugely', 'immensely', 'moderately', 'adequately', 'greatly', 'strongly', 'tremendously', 'profoundly', 'totally', 'entirely', 'perfectly', 'partially', 'practically', 'virtually', 'almost', as in 'They enjoyed the show hugely', 'The office was not adequately equipped', 'We strongly disapprove of such behaviour', 'He was totally unaware of the facts', 'They are virtually penniless'.

An **adverb of frequency** is used to tell us how often something happens, and they include 'never', 'rarely', 'seldom', 'infrequently', 'occasionally', 'periodically', 'intermittently', 'sometimes', 'often', 'frequently', 'regularly', 'normally', 'always', 'constantly', 'continually', as in 'She never eats breakfast', 'We go to the cinema occasionally', 'He goes to the dentist regularly', 'Normally they travel by bus', 'He is in pain constantly'.

An **adverb of probability** tells us how often something happens, and they include 'probably', 'possibly', 'conceivably', 'perhaps', 'maybe', 'presumably', 'hopefully', 'definitely', 'certainly', 'indubitably', 'doubtless', as in 'You will probably see them there', 'He may conceivably pass the exam this time', 'Presumably they know that she is leaving', 'Hopefully the news will be good', 'I am definitely not going', 'He is indubitably a criminal'.

An **adverb of duration** tells us how long something takes or lasts, and they include 'briefly', 'temporarily', 'long', 'indefinitely', 'always', 'permanently', 'forever', as in 'We stopped briefly for coffee', 'Have you known her long?', 'Her face is permanently disfigured', 'They have parted forever'.

An **adverb of emphasis** adds emphasis to the action described by the verb, and they include 'absolutely', 'certainly', 'positively', 'quite', 'really', 'simply', 'just', as in 'They absolutely detest each other', 'He positively adores her', 'She really wants to be forgiven', 'I simply must go now'

An **interrogative adverb** asks questions, and they include 'where', 'when', 'how', and 'why', as in 'Where are you going?', 'When will you be back?', 'How will you get there?', 'Why have they asked you to go?' They are placed at the beginning of sentences, and such sentences always end with a question mark.

adverbial clause

A subordinate clause that modifies the main or principal clause by adding information about time, place, concession, condition, manner, purpose and result. Adverbial clauses usually follow the main clause but most of them can be put in front of the main clause for reasons of emphasis or style.

An **adverbial clause of time** indicates the time of an event and is introduced by a conjunction such as 'after', 'as', 'as soon as', 'before', 'once', 'since', 'the minute', 'the moment', 'till', 'until', 'when', 'whenever, while', 'whilst', as in 'He left after the meal was over', 'She arrived as I was leaving', 'Once I recognized him I spoke to him', 'I recognized him the minute I saw him', 'We won't know until tomorrow' and 'The thief ran away when he saw the police'.

An **adverbial clause of place** indicates the location of an event and is introduced by a conjunction such as 'where', 'wherever' or 'everywhere', as in 'He was miserable where he was', 'They left it where they found it', 'Wherever I went I saw signs of poverty' and 'Everywhere she goes she causes trouble'.

An **adverbial clause of concession** contains a fact that contrasts in some way with the main clause and is introduced by a CONJUNCTION such as 'although', 'even though', 'though', 'whereas', 'while', 'whilst', as in 'I have to admire his speech, although I disagree with what he said', 'He does his best at school work even though he is not very good at it' and 'Whilst I myself do not like him I can understand why he is popular'.

An **adverbial clause of condition** deals with possible situations and is introduced by the conjunctions 'if', 'only if', 'unless', 'as long as', 'providing', 'provided', as in 'If you had kept quiet they would not have known about the event', 'We cannot go unless we get permission', 'They can leave only if they have finished their work' and 'Provided he is feeling better he can leave hospital'. Inversion can be used in such clauses instead of a conjunction, as in 'Had you been present you would have been most amused' and 'Had he any sense he would leave now'.

An **adverbial clause of manner** describes the way that someone behaves or the way in which something is done, and is introduced by a conjunction such as 'as', 'as if', 'as though', 'like', 'the way', as in 'Why does he behave as he does', 'He slurred his speech as though he were drunk' and 'He looked at her as if he hated her'.

An **adverbial clause of purpose** indicates the intention someone has when doing something and is introduced by a conjunction such as 'to', 'in order to', 'so as to', 'so', 'so that', as in 'He did that just to upset her', 'They will have to work long hours in order to make that amount of money', 'They started to run so as to get home before it rained' and 'The firm reduced the number of staff in order that they might avoid bankruptcy'.

An **adverbial clause of reason** explains why something happens or is done and is introduced by a conjunction such as 'because', 'since' or 'as', as in 'We didn't go because the car broke down', 'As it was raining we had the party indoors' and 'since he has broken the school rules he should be punished'.

An **adverbial clause of result** indicates the result of an event or situation and is introduced by the conjunctions 'so' or 'so that', as in 'He fell awkwardly so that he broke his leg' and 'She stumbled over her words so that the audience had difficulty understanding her'. See COMPARISON OF ADVERBS and COMPOUNDS.

aero-
A prefix meaning 'air', as in aerobics, aerodynamics, aeroplane and aerospace, or 'aircraft', as in aerodrome, aeronaut.

affix
An element that is added to a base or root word to form another word. Affixes can be in the form of prefixes or suffixes. A **prefix** is an affix that is added to the beginning of a word. Thus *audio* in 'audiovisual' is both a prefix and an affix. A **suffix** is an affix that is added to the end of a word. Thus *-aholic* in 'workaholic' is a suffix and an affix.

agent noun
A noun that refers to someone who is the 'doer' of the action of a verb. It is usually spelt ending in either *-er*, as 'enquirer', or in *-or*, as in 'investigator' and 'supervisor', but frequently either of these endings is acceptable, as 'adviser/advisor'.

agreement or concord
The agreeing of two or more elements in a clause or sentence, i.e. they take the same number, person or gender. In English the most common form of agreement is that between subject and verb, and this usually involves NUMBER AGREEMENT. This means that singular nouns are usually accompanied by singular

verbs, as in 'She looks well', 'He is working late' and 'The boy has passed the exam', and that plural nouns are usually accompanied by plural verbs, as in 'They look well', 'They are working late' and 'The boys have passed the exam'.

Problems arise when the noun in question can be either singular or plural, for example, 'audience', 'committee', 'crowd', 'family', 'government', 'group'. Such nouns take a singular verb if the user is regarding the people or items referred to by the noun as a group, as in 'The family is moving house', or as individuals, as in 'The family are quarrelling over where to go on holiday'.

Compound subjects, that is two or more nouns acting as the subject, whether singular or plural, joined with 'and', are used with a plural noun, as in 'My friend and I are going to the cinema tonight' and 'James and John are leaving today', unless the two nouns together represent a single concept, as 'brandy and soda', in which case the verb is in the singular, as in 'Brandy and soda is his favourite drink' and 'cheese and pickle' in 'Cheese and pickle is the only sandwich filling available'.

In cases where two or more singular nouns acting as the subject are connected with such phrases as 'as well as', 'together with' and 'plus', as in 'His mother, as well as his father, is away from home' and 'The flat, together with the house, is up for sale', the verb is in the singular.

Indefinite pronouns such as 'anyone', 'everyone', 'no one', 'someone', 'either', 'neither' are singular and should be followed by a singular verb, as in 'Each of the flats is self-contained', 'Everyone is welcome', 'No one is allowed in without a ticket' and 'Neither is quite what I am looking for'.

When the subject is a singular noun, which is separated from the verb by a number of plural nouns, as in 'a list of dates and times of the next concerts', the verb is in the singular because 'list' is singular, as in 'A list of dates and times of the next concerts is available'.

Agreement with reference to both number and gender affects pronouns, as in 'She blames herself', 'He could have kicked himself' and 'They asked themselves why they had got involved'. Problems arise when the pronoun is indefinite and so the sex of the person is unspecified. Formerly in such cases the masculine pronouns were assumed to be neutral and so 'Each of the pupils was asked to hand in his work' was considered quite acceptable. The rise of feminism has led to a questioning of this assumption and alternatives have been put forward. These include 'Each of the pupils was asked to hand in his/her (or his or her) work', but some people feel that this is clumsy. Another alternative is 'Each of the pupils was asked to hand in their work'. Although it is ungrammatical, this convention is becoming quite acceptable in modern usage. To avoid both the clumsiness of the former and the ungrammaticalness of the latter, it is possible to cast the whole sentence in the plural, as in 'All the pupils were asked to hand in their work'.

agro-, agri-
A prefix derived from Greek meaning 'field', as in agriculture, agribusiness, agrobiology, agrochemicals.

-aholic
A suffix meaning 'addicted to', formed on ANALOGY with 'alcoholic', as in workaholic, shopaholic. It sometimes becomes -**oholic**, as in chocoholic.

allegory

A kind of story that has deeper significance as well as the obvious surface meaning of the story. It is usually used to get a moral message across symbolically. Two of the most famous allegories in English literature are *The Pilgrim's Progress* by John Bunyan (1628-88) and *The Faerie Queene* by Edmund Spenser (c.1552-99).

alliteration

A figure of speech in which a sequence of words begin with the same letter or sound, as in 'Round and round the rugged rocks the ragged rascal ran' and 'Peter Piper picked a peck of pickled peppers'. The given examples are both tongue twisters but alliteration is frequently used by poets for literary effect as in a 'red, red rose'.

also

An adverb that should not be used as a CONJUNCTION instead of 'and'. Thus sentences such as 'Please send me some apples, also some pears' are grammatically incorrect.

although

A conjunction that is used to introduce a subordinate adverbial clause of concession, as in 'They are very happy although they are poor', meaning 'Despite the fact they are poor they are happy'. 'Though' or 'even though' can be substituted for 'although', as in 'they are very happy even though they are poor'. *See* ADVERBIAL CLAUSE and CONJUNCTION.

ambi-

A prefix derived from Greek 'two', 'both', as in ambidextrous, ambivalent.

an see **indefinite article**.

an- see **a-**.

-ana

A suffix meaning 'things associated with', as in Victoriana, Americana.

anacoluthon

A FIGURE OF SPEECH that refers to a change of construction in a sentence before the original structure is complete, as in 'My feeling is—but you must decide for yourself—how long did you say you have?' Anacoluthon is usually found in spoken English when someone is thinking aloud. Unlike many figures of speech, it is usually used accidentally rather than for literary or rhetorical effect.

anadiplosis

A FIGURE OF SPEECH that refers to the repetition of a word or group at the end of one phrase or sentence and the beginning of the next for literary effect, as in 'sit and think about the past—the past which had been so warm and happy'.

analogy

A FIGURE OF SPEECH, rather like the SIMILE, in which there is an inference of a resemblance between two items that are being compared, as in 'Mary's parties are a bit like Christmas—much looked forward to but often a bit of a disappointment'.

anastrophe

A FIGURE OF SPEECH that refers to an inversion of the usual order of words in a sentence or phrase for emphasis, or literary or rhetorical effect, as in 'Many a foreign dawn has he seen'.

and

A conjunction that is called a coordinating conjunction because it joins elements of language that are of equal status. The elements may be words, as in 'cows and horses', 'John and James', 'provide wine and beer'; phrases, as in 'working hard and playing hard' and 'trying to look after her children and her elderly parents'; clauses, as in 'John has decided to emigrate and his brother has decided to join him' and 'He has lost his job and he now has no money'. When a coordinating conjunction is used, the subject of the second clause can sometimes be omitted if it is the same as the subject of the first clause, as in 'They have been forced to sell the house and are very sad about it'. See CONJUNCTION.

The use of and at the beginning of a sentence is disliked by many people. It should be used only for deliberate effect, as in 'And then he saw the monster', or in informal contexts.

Other coordinating conjunctions include 'but', 'or', 'yet', 'both... and', 'either... or', and 'neither.... nor', as in 'poor but honest' and 'the blue dress or the green one'.

Anglo-

A prefix meaning 'English', as in Anglo-Irish, Anglo-Indian.

ante-

A prefix derived from Latin meaning 'before', as in antedate, antenatal, anteroom.

antecedent

A term that refers to the noun or noun phrase in a main clause to which a relative pronoun in a relative clause refers back. Thus in the sentence 'People who live dangerously frequently get hurt', 'people' is an antecedent. Similarly, in the sentence 'The child identified the old man who attacked her', 'the old man' is the antecedent. *See* RELATIVE CLAUSE.

anthropo-

A prefix derived from Greek meaning 'human being', as in anthropoid, anthropology.

anti-

A prefix derived from Greek meaning 'against'. It is used in many words that have been established in the language for a long time, as in antidote and antipathy, but it has also been used to form modern words, such as anti-establishment, antifreeze, anti-inflationary, anti-nuclear, anti-warfare.

anticlimax

A FIGURE OF SPEECH in which there is a sudden descent from the lofty to the ridiculous or the trivial, as in 'She went home in a flood of tears and a taxi'. A well-known 19th-century example is in the couplet:
'And thou, Dalhousie, the great god of war,
Lieutenant-general to the earl of Mar'.

antiphrasis

A FIGURE OF SPEECH in which a word or phrase is used in a sense that is opposite to the accepted sense. It is often used to achieve an ironic or humorous effect, as in 'His mother is ninety years young today'. Young is usually associated with youth but here it is associated with old age.

antithesis

A FIGURE OF SPEECH in which contrasting ideas are balanced for effect, as in 'We need money, not advice', 'More haste, less speed' and 'Marry at haste, repent at leisure'. It is a common figure of speech in literature, as in Alexander Pope's 'To err is human, to forgive, divine' and John Milton's 'Better to reign in hell than to serve in heaven'.

antonomasia

A FIGURE OF SPEECH indicating the use of a personal name or proper name to anyone belonging to a class or group, as in 'John is such an Einstein that the other members of the class are in awe of him', where the meaning is that 'John has such a brilliant mind that the other members of the class are in awe of him'.

antonym

A word that is the opposite of another word. Thus 'black' is an antonym for 'white', 'cowardly' is an antonym for 'courageous', 'dull' is an antonym for 'bright', and 'fast' is an antonym for 'slow'.

any

A pronoun that may take either a singular or plural verb, depending on the context. When a singular noun is used, a singular verb is used, as in 'Is any of the cloth still usable?' 'Are any of the children coming?' When a plural noun is used, either a plural or a singular verb can be used, the singular verb being more formal, as in 'Did you ask if any of his friends were/was there?'.

anyone

A pronoun that should be used with a singular verb, as in 'Has anyone seen my book?' and 'Is anyone coming to the lecture?' It should also be followed, where relevant, by a singular, not plural, personal pronoun or possessive adjective, as in 'Has anyone left his/her book?' Because this construction, which avoids the sexist 'his', is considered by many people to be clumsy, there is a growing tendency to use 'their' and be ungrammatical.

aposiopesis

A FIGURE OF SPEECH in which words are omitted or there is a sudden breaking off for dramatic effect, as in 'The door slowly opened and....' and 'There was the noise of gunshot and then....'

apostrophe[1]

A FIGURE OF SPEECH that takes the form of a rhetorical address to an absent or dead person or to a personified thing, as in 'O Romeo! Romeo! wherefore art thou, Romeo?' and 'Oh Peace, why have you deserted us?'

apostrophe[2]

A form of punctuation that is mainly used to indicate possession. Many spelling errors centre on the position of the apostrophe in relation to s.

Possessive nouns are usually formed by adding 's to the singular noun, as in 'the girl's mother', and Peter's car'; by adding an apostrophe to plural nouns that end in s, as in 'all the teachers' cars'; by adding 's to irregular plural nouns that do not end in s, as in 'women's shoes'.

In the possessive form of a name or singular noun that ends in s, x or z, the apostrophe may or may not be followed by s. In words of one syllable the final s is usually added, as in 'James's house', 'the fox's lair', 'Roz's dress'. The final s is most frequently omitted in names, particularly in names of three or more syllables, as in 'Euripides' plays'. In many cases the presence or absence of final *s* is a matter of convention.

The apostrophe is also used to indicate omitted letters in contracted forms of words, as in 'can't' and 'you've'. They are sometimes used to indicate missing century numbers in dates, as in 'the '60s and '70s', but are not used at the end of decades, etc, as in '1960s', not '1960's'.

Generally apostrophes are no longer used to indicate omitted letters in shortened forms that are in common use, as in 'phone' and 'flu'.

Apostrophes are often omitted wrongly in modern usage, particularly in the media and by advertisers, as in 'womens hairdressers', 'childrens helpings'. In addition, apostrophes are frequently added erroneously (as in 'potato's for sale' and 'Beware of the dog's'). This is partly because people are unsure about when and when not to use them and partly because of a modern tendency to punctuate as little as possible.

apposition
A term for a noun or a phrase that provides further information about another noun or phrase. Both nouns and phrases refer to the same person or thing. In the phrase 'Peter Jones, our managing director', ' Peter Jones' and 'our managing director' are said to be in apposition. Similarly, in the phrase 'his cousin, the chairman of the firm', 'his cousin' and 'the chairman of the firm' are in apposition.

arch-
A prefix derived from Greek meaning 'chief', as in archbishop, archduke, arch-enemy.

-arch

A suffix derived from the Greek meaning 'chief, ruler', as in anarchy, hierarchy and monarchy.

-arian

A suffix derived from Latin that means, in one of its senses, 'a supporter of', as in vegetarian, or 'one connected with', as in antiquarian and librarian.

article see **definite article** and **indefinite article**.

as

A conjunction that can introduce either a subordinate adverbial clause of time, as in 'I caught sight of him as I was leaving', a subordinate adverbial clause of manner, as in 'He acted as he promised', and a subordinate adverbial clause of reason, as in 'As it's Saturday he doesn't have to work'. it is also used in the as....as construction, as in 'She doesn't play as well as her sister does'.

The construction may be followed by a subject pronoun or an object pronoun, according to sense. In the sentence 'He plays as well as she', which is a slightly shortened form of 'She plays as well as he does', 'he' is a subject pronoun. In informal English the subject pronoun often becomes an object pronoun, as in 'She plays as well as him'. In the sentence 'They hate their father as much as her', 'her' is an object and the sentence means 'They hate their father as much as they hate her', but in the sentence 'They hate their father as much as she', 'she' is a subject and the sentence means 'They hate their father as much as she does'. See ADVERBIAL CLAUSE and CONJUNCTION.

assonance
A figure of speech in which vowel sounds are repeated to give a half-rhyme effect, as in 'with gun, drum, trumpet, blunderbuss and thunder'.

astro-
A prefix derived from Greek meaning 'star', as in astrology, astronomy, astronaut, astrophysics.

asyndeton
A figure of speech referring to the omission of conjunctions for dramatic or literary effect, as in 'I came, I saw, I conquered' and 'He entered, he looked round, he left'.

-athon, -thon
A suffix meaning 'large scale or long-lasting contest or event', as in swimathon, telethon. These words are formed on analogy with the Greek derived word marathon, and they often refer to events undertaken for charity.

attributive adjective
A term for an adjective that is placed immediately before the noun that it qualifies. In the phrases 'a red dress', 'the big house' and 'an enjoyable evening', 'red, 'big' and 'enjoyable' are attributive adjectives.

audio-
A word derived from the Latin 'hear'. It is found in several words that have been established in the language for a long time, as in auditory, audition, but it is also used to form many modern words, as in audiotape, audio-cassette and audio-visual.

auto-

A prefix derived from Greek meaning 'of or by itself', as in autobiography and autograph. It is also used to refer to things that work by themselves 'automatically', as in automobile, autocue, automaton, and to things that have to do with cars, as in automobiles, autosport, autotheft.

auxiliary verb

A verb that is used in forming tenses, moods and voices of other verbs. These include 'be', 'do' and 'have'.

The verb 'to be' is used as an **auxiliary verb** with the *-ing* form of the main verb to form the continuous present tense, as in 'They are living abroad just now' and 'We were thinking of going on holiday but we changed our minds'.

The verb 'to be' is used as an auxiliary verb with the past participle of the main verb to form the passive voice, as in 'Her hands were covered in blood' and 'These toys are manufactured in China'.

The verb 'to have' is used as an auxiliary verb along with the past participle of the main verb to form the perfect tenses, as in 'They have filled the post', 'She had realized her mistake' and 'They wished that they had gone earlier'.

The verb 'to be' is used as an auxiliary verb along with the main verb to form negative sentences, as in 'She is not accepting the job'. The verb 'to do' is used as an auxiliary verb along with the main verb to form negative sentences, as in 'he does not believe her'. It is also used along with the main verb to form questions, as in 'Does he know that she's gone?' and to form sentences in which the verb is emphasized, as in 'She *does* want to go'. See MODAL VERB.

B

back formation

The process of forming a new word by removing an element from an existing word. This is the reversal of the usual process since many words are formed by adding an element to a base or root word. Examples of back formation include 'burgle' from 'burglary'; 'caretake' from 'caretaker'; 'donate' from 'donation; 'eavesdrop' from 'eavesdropper'; 'enthuse' from 'enthusiasm'; 'intuit' from 'intuition'; 'liaise' from 'liaison'; 'reminisce' from 'reminiscence'; 'televise' from 'television'.

base

The basic uninflected form of a verb. It is found as the infinitive form, as in 'to go' and 'to take', and as the imperative form, as in 'Go away!' and 'Take it!' It is also the form that the verb in the present indicative tense takes, except for the third person singular, as in 'I always go there on a Sunday' and 'They go there regularly.'

   Base also refers to the basic element in word formation. In this sense it is also known as 'root' or 'stem'. For example, in the word 'infectious' 'infect' is the base, in 'indescribable' 'describe' is the base and in 'enthusiastic' 'enthuse' is the base.

bathos

A figure of speech consisting of sudden descent from the lofty or noble to the ridiculous or trivial. This descent can be either intentional for comic or satiric effect, as in Alexander Pope's 'When husbands or when lapdogs breathe their last', or it can be accidental, as in 'She collected her children and her coat'. Bathos and anticlimax mean the same. See ANTICLIMAX.

be see **auxiliary verb**.

both

A word that can be used in several ways: as a determiner, as in 'He broke both his arms' and 'He lost both his sons in the war'; as a pronoun, as in 'I don't mind which house we rent, I like them both' and 'Neither of them work here. The boss sacked them both'; as a conjunction, as in 'He both likes and admires her' and 'She is both talented and honest'. Both can sometimes be followed by 'of'. 'Both their children are grown up' and 'Both of their children are grown up' are both acceptable. Care should be taken to avoid using both unnecessarily. In the sentence 'The two items are both identical', 'both' is redundant.

because

A conjunction that introduces a subordinate adverbial clause of reason, as in 'They sold the house because they are going abroad' and 'Because she is shy she never goes to parties'. It is often used incorrectly in such constructions as 'The reason they went away is because they were bored'. This should be rephrased as either 'The reason that they went away is that they were bored' or 'They went away because they were bored'. See ADVERBIAL CLAUSE.

before

A word that can either be a preposition, an adverb or a conjunction. As a preposition it means either 'coming or going in front of in time', as in 'He was the chairman before this one', or coming or going in front of in place, as in 'She went before him into the restaurant'. As an adverb it means 'at a time previously', as in 'I told you before' and 'He has been married before'. As a conjunction it introduces a subordinate adverbial clause of time, as in 'The guests arrived before she was ready for them' and 'Before I knew it they had arrived'. See ADVERBIAL CLAUSE.

bi-

A prefix that is derived from Latin meaning 'two', as in bicycle, bifocal, bilingual, binoculars, bisect. Bi- forms words in English in which it means 'half', and other words in which it means 'twice'. This can give rise to confusion in such words as biweekly and bimonthly, where there are two possible sets of meanings. Biweekly can mean either 'every two weeks' or 'twice a week' so that one would not be able to be certain about the frequency of a 'biweekly publication'. Similarly, a 'bimonthly publication' might appear either twice a month or once every two months.

biblio-

A prefix derived from Greek meaning 'book', as in bibliophile (a person who is fond of or collects books) and bibliography.

bio-

A prefix derived from Greek meaning life or living material, as in biography, biology, biochemistry, biodegradable, biosphere, biopsy.

blend
A word that is formed by the merging of two other words or elements, as in 'brunch' from 'breakfast' and 'lunch'; 'camcorder' from 'camera' and 'recorder'; 'chocoholic' from 'chocolate' and 'alcoholic'; 'motel' from 'motor' and 'hotel'; 'smog' from 'smoke' and 'fog'; 'televangelist' from 'television' and 'evangelist'.

bold or **bold face**
A typeface that is thick and black. It is used for emphasis or to highlight certain words. The headwords, or entry words, in this book are set in bold type.

book titles
These can cause problems as to punctuation. How they are treated in publications, business reports, etc, depends largely on the house style of the firm concerned. However, they are generally written in documents, letters, etc, as they appear on their title pages, that is with the first letter of the first word and of the following main words of the title in capital letters, and those of words of lesser importance, such as the articles, prepositions and coordinate conjunctions, in lowercase letters, as in The Guide to Yoga, Hope for the Best and In the Middle of Life.

Some people, and some house-style manuals, prefer to put the titles in italic, as in *A Room with a View* and *A Guide to Dental Health*. Others prefer to put book titles in quotation marks, as in 'Gardening for Beginners'. Such a convention can make use of either single or double quotation marks. Thus either 'Desserts for the Summer' or "Desserts for the Summer" is possible provided that the writer is consistent throughout any one piece of writing. If the title of a book is mentioned in a piece of direct speech in quotation marks it goes within the opposite style of quotation marks from the piece in direct speech. Thus if the direct speech is within single quotation marks, the book title goes within double quotation marks, as in 'Have you read "Wuthering Heights" or are you not a Bronte fan?' If the direct speech is within double quotation marks, the book title goes between single quotation marks, as in "Would you say that 'Animal Farm' was your favourite Orwell novel?"

It is even quite common for book titles to appear in documents both in italic type and with quotation marks. To some extent the punctuation of book titles is a matter of choice as long as they are consistent, but there is a growing tendency to have as little punctuation as possible and to have as uncluttered a page as possible.

borrowing

The taking over into English of a word from a foreign language and also to the word so borrowed. Many words borrowed into English are totally assimilated as to spelling and pronunciation. Others remain obviously different and retain their own identity as to spelling or pronunciation, as *raison d'être*, borrowed from French. Many of them have been so long part of the English language, such as since the Norman Conquest, that they are no longer thought of as being foreign words. However the process goes on, and recent borrowings include *glasnost* and *perestroika* from Russian.

French, Latin and Greek have been the main sources of our borrowings over the centuries. However, we have borrowed extensively from other languages as well. These include Italian, from which we have borrowed many terms relating to music, art and architecture. These include *piano, libretto, opera, soprano, tempo, corridor, fresco, niche, parapet* and *grotto,* as well as many food terms, such as *macaroni, pasta, semolina* and *spaghetti.*

From the Dutch we have acquired many words relating to the sea and ships since they were a great sea-faring nation. These include *cruise, deck, skipper* and *yacht.* Through the Dutch/Afrikaans connection we have borrowed *apartheid, boss* and *trek.*

From German we have borrowed *dachshund, hamster, frankfurter, kindergarten* and *waltz,* as well as some words relating to World War II, for example, *blitz, flak* and *strafe.*

From Norse and the Scandinavian languages have come a wide variety of common words, such as *egg, dirt, glitter, kick, law, odd, skill, take, they, though,* as well as some more modern sporting terms such as *ski* and *slalom.*

From the Celtic languages have come *bannock, bog, brogue, cairn, clan, crag, slogan* and *whisky,* and from Arabic have come *algebra, alkali, almanac, apricot, assassin, cypher, ghoul, hazard, mohair, safari, scarlet* and *talisman.*

The Indian languages have provided us with many words, originally from the significant British presence there in the days of the British Empire. They include *bungalow, chutney, dinghy, dungarees, gymkhana, jungle, pundit* and *shampoo.* In modern times there has been an increasing interest in Indian food and cookery, and words such as *pakora, poppadom, samosa,* etc, have come into the language.

From the South American languages have come *avocado,*

chocolate, chilli, potato, tobacco and *tomato*. From Hebrew have come *alphabet, camel, cinnamon* and *maudlin*, as well as more modern borrowings from Yiddish such as *bagel, chutzpah, schmaltz* and *schmuck*.

From the native North American languages have come *anorak, kayak, raccoon* and *toboggan*, and from the Aboriginal language of Australia have come *boomerang* and *kangaroo*.

Judo, bonsai and *tycoon* have come from Japanese, *rattan* from Malay and *kung-fu, sampan* and *ginseng* from Chinese.

The borrowing process continues. With Britain becoming more of a cosmopolitan and multi-cultural nation the borrowing is increasing.

-bound

A suffix meaning 'confined or restricted', as in housebound, snowbound and spellbound. It can also mean 'obligated', as in duty-bound.

brackets

A pair of characters that are used to enclose information that is in some way additional to a main statement. The information so enclosed is called **parenthesis** and the pair of brackets enclosing it can be known as **parentheses**. The information that is enclosed in the brackets is purely supplementary or explanatory in nature and could be removed without changing the overall basic meaning or grammatical completeness of the statement. Brackets, like commas and dashes, interrupt the flow of the main statement but brackets indicate a more definite or clear-cut interruption. The fact that they are more visually obvious emphasizes this.

Material within brackets can be one word, as in 'In a local wine bar we had some delicious crepes (pancakes)' and 'They didn't have the chutzpah (nerve) to challenge her'. It can also take the form of dates, as in 'Robert Louis Stevenson (1850-94) wrote *Treasure Island*' and '*Animal Farm* was written by George Orwell (1903-50)'.

The material within brackets can also take the form of a phrase, as in 'They served lasagne (a kind of pasta) and some delicious veal' and 'They were drinking Calvados (a kind of brandy made from apples)' or in the form of a clause, as in 'We were to have supper (or so they called it) later in the evening' and 'They went for a walk round the loch (as a lake is called in Scotland) before taking their departure'.

It can also take the form of a complete sentence, as in 'He was determined (we don't know why) to tackle the problem alone' and 'She made it clear (nothing could be more clear) that she was not interested in the offer'. Sentences that appear in brackets in the middle of a sentence are not usually given an initial capital letter or a full stop, as in 'They very much desired (she had no idea why) to purchase her house'. If the material within brackets comes at the end of a sentence the full stop comes outside the second bracket, as in 'For some reason we agreed to visit her at home (we had no idea where she lived)'.

If the material in the brackets is a sentence which comes between two other sentences it is treated like a normal sentence with an initial capital letter and a closing full stop, as in 'He never seems to do any studying. (He is always either asleep or watching television.) Yet he does brilliantly in his exams.' Punctuation of the main statement is unaffected by the presence of the brackets and their enclosed material except that any punctuation that would have followed the word before the first bracket follows the second bracket, as in 'He lives in a place (I am not sure exactly where), that is miles from anywhere.

There are various shapes of brackets. Round brackets are the most common type. Square brackets are sometimes used to enclose information that is contained inside other information already in brackets, as in '(Christopher Marlowe [1564-93] was a contemporary of Shakespeare)' or in a piece of writing where round brackets have already been used for some other purpose. Thus in a dictionary if round brackets are used to separate off the pronunciation, square brackets are sometimes used to separate off the etymologies.

Square brackets are also used for editorial comments in a scholarly work where the material within brackets is more of an intrusion to the flow of the main statement than is normerly the case with bracketed material. Angle brackets and brace brackets tend to be used in more scholarly or technical contexts.

buildings

These can cause problems with regard to the style and punctuation of their names. The proper name attached to the building should have an initial capital, as should the common noun that may be part of it, as in The White House, The Saltire Building, The National Portrait Gallery and The Museum of Childhood.

businesses and organizations

These often cause style and punctuation problems with regard to their names or titles. In general the initial letters of the main words of the title should be in capital letters and the words of lesser importance, such as the articles, coordinating conjunctions and prepositions, should be in lower case, except when they are the first word of the title, as in 'The Indian Carpet Company', 'Kitchens for All' and 'Capital Industrial Cleaners'. Obviously, when the names of people are involved these should have initial capital letters, as in 'Jones and Brown'.

but

A conjunction that connects two opposing ideas. It is a coordinating conjunction in that it connects two elements of equal status. The elements may be words, as in 'not James but John'; phrases, as in 'working hard but not getting anywhere' and 'trying to earn a living but not succeeding'; clauses, as in 'He has arrived but his sister is late', 'I know her but I have never met him' and 'He likes reading but she prefers to watch TV'. It should not be used when no element of contrast is present. Thus the following sentence should be rephrased, at least in formal English—'She is not professionally trained but taught herself'. The two clauses are in fact agreeing, not disagreeing, with each other and so, strictly speaking, but should not be used.

The use of but at the beginning of a sentence is disliked by many people. It should be used only for deliberate effect or in informal contexts.

by-

A prefix meaning 'subordinate', 'secondary', 'incidental', as in by-product, by-road, by-effect. It can also mean 'around', as in by-pass.

C

capital letters
These are much less common than lower-case letters. They are used as the initial letters of proper nouns, the names of countries, rivers, mountains, cities, etc. Thus we find Africa, Mount Everest, River Nile, Paris, etc. The first names and surnames of people have initial capital letters, as in John Black and Mary Brown. Initial capital letters are used for the days of the week, as in Tuesday and Wednesday, for the months of the year, as in May and October, public and religious holidays, as in Easter Sunday, Ramadan and Hanaku. Initial capital letters are used for the books of the Bible.

Points of the compass are spelt with an initial capital letter if they are part of a specific geographical feature or region, as in South Africa.

Initial capital letters are usually used in the titles of books. Only the main words are capitalized. Prepositions, determiners and the articles are left in lower-case unless they form the first word of the title, as in *A Room with a View* and *For Whom the Bell Tolls*—SEE BOOK TITLES.

Initial capital letters are necessary in tradenames, as in Hoover, Jacuzzi, Xerox and Kodak. Note that verbs formed from trade names are not spelt with an initial capital letter.

The first word in a sentence is spelt with a capital letter, as in 'We heard them come in. They made very little noise. However, we are light sleepers.'

cardi-

For capital letters in direct speech, see DIRECT SPEECH. For capital letters in abbreviation and acronyms, see ABBREVIATION and ACRONYM.

cardi-
A prefix derived from Greek meaning 'heart', as in cardiology, cardiac.

cardinal number
The numbers one, two three, four, etc, as opposed to ORDINAL NUMBERS, which refer to numbers such as first, second, third, fourth, etc.

case
One of the forms in the DECLENSION of a noun, pronoun or adjective in a sentence.

clause
A group of words containing a FINITE VERB which forms part of a compound or complex sentence. See MAIN CLAUSE, SUBORDINATE CLAUSES, ADVERBIAL CLAUSE, NOUN CLAUSE and RELATIVE CLAUSE.

clerihew
A humorous four-line light verse in which the first two lines rhyme with each other and the last two rhyme with each other. The clerihew was popularized by Edward Clerihew Bentley (1875-1956). It usually deals with a person named in the first line and then describes him in a humorous way, as in

    Mr Michael Foot
    Had lots of loot
    He loved to gloat
    While petting his stoat

cliché

A hackneyed stereotyped expression that is much overused. Examples of clichés include 'unaccustomed as I am to public speaking', 'the light at the end of the tunnel' and 'All's well that ends well'.

collective noun

A singular noun that refers to a group of things or people. It is used when the whole group is being considered, as in 'flock of sheep', 'herd of cattle', 'team of oxen', 'shoal of herring', 'covey of partridges', 'unkindness of ravens', 'gaggle of geese', 'pride of lions', 'mutation of thrushes', 'exaltation of larks', 'convocation of eagles'.

colloquial

A term used to describe informal language, such as that found in informal conversation.

colon

A punctuation mark (:) that is used within a sentence to explain, interpret, clarify or amplify what has gone before it. 'The standard of school work here is extremely high: it is almost university standard', 'The fuel bills are giving cause for concern: they are almost double last year's'. 'We have some new information: the allies have landed'. A capital letter is not usually used after the colon in this context.

The colon is also used to introduce lists or long quotations, as in 'The recipe says we need: tomatoes, peppers, courgettes, garlic, oregano and basil', 'The boy has a huge list of things he needs for school: blazer, trousers, shirts, sweater, ties, shoes, tennis shoes, rugby boots, sports clothes and leisure wear' and 'One of his favourite quotations was: "If music be the food of love play on".'

The colon is sometimes used in numerals, as in '7:30 a.m.', '22:11:72' and 'a ratio of 7:3'. It is used in the titles of some books, for example where there is a subtitle or explanatory title, as in 'The Dark Years: the Economy in the 1930s'.

In informal writing, the dash is sometimes used instead of the colon, Indeed the dash tends to be overused for this purpose.

comma

A very common punctuation mark (,). In modern usage there is a tendency to adopt a system of minimal punctuation and the comma is one of the casualties of this new attitude. Most people use the comma considerably less frequently than was formerly the case.

However there are certain situations in which the comma is still commonly used. One of these concerns lists. The individual items in a series of three or more items are separated by commas. Whether a comma is put before the 'and' which follows the second-last item is now a matter of choice. Some people dislike the use of a comma before 'and' in this situation, and it was formerly considered wrong. Examples of lists include—'at the sports club we can play tennis, squash, badminton and table tennis', 'We need to buy bread, milk, fruit and sugar', and 'They are studying French, German, Spanish and Russian'. The individual items in a list can be quite long, as in 'We opened the door, let ourselves in, fed the cat and started to cook a meal' and 'They consulted the map, planned the trip, got some foreign currency and were gone before we realized it'. Confusion may arise if the last item in the list contains 'and' in its own right, as in 'In the pub they served ham salad, shepherd's pie, pie and chips and omelette'. In such cases it as well to put a comma before the final 'and'.

In cases where there is a list of adjectives before a noun, the use of commas is now optional although it was formerly standard practice. Thus both 'She wore a long, red, sequinned dress' and 'She wore a long red sequinned dress' are used. When the adjective immediately before the noun has a closer relationship with it than the other adjectives no comma should be used, as in 'a beautiful old Spanish village'.

The comma is used to separate clauses or phrases that are parenthetical or naturally cut off from the rest of a sentence, as in 'My mother, who was of Irish extraction, was very superstitious'. In such a sentence the clause within the commas can be removed without altering the basic meaning. Care should be taken to include both commas. Commas are not normally used to separate main clauses and relative clauses, as in 'The woman whom I met was my friend's sister'. Nor are they usually used to separate main clauses and subordinate clauses, as in 'He left when we arrived' and 'They came to the party although we didn't expect them to'. If the subordinate clause precedes the main clause, it is sometimes followed by a comma, especially if it is a reasonably long clause, as in 'Although we stopped and thought about it, we still made the wrong decision'. If the clause is quite short, or if it is a short phrase, a comma is not usually inserted, as in 'Although it rained we had a good holiday' and 'Although poor they were happy'. The use of commas to separate such words and expression from the rest of the sentence to which they are related is optional. Thus one can write 'However, he could be right' or 'However he could be right'. The longer the expression is, the more likely it is to have a comma after it, as in 'On the other hand, we may decide not to go'.

Commas are always used to separate terms of address, interjections or question tags from the rest of the sentence, as in 'Please come this way, Ms Brown, and make yourself at home', 'Now, ladies, what can I get you?' and 'It's cold today, isn't it?'

Commas may be used to separate main clauses joined by a coordinating conjunction, but this is not usual if the clauses have the same subject or object, as in 'She swept the floor and dusted the table'. In cases where the subjects are different and the clauses are fairly long, it is best to insert a comma, as in 'They took all the furniture with them, and she was left with nothing'.

A comma can be inserted to avoid repeating a verb in the second of two clause, as in 'he plays golf and tennis, his brother rugby'.

commands

These are expressed in the imperative mood, as in 'Be quiet!', 'Stop crying!', 'Go away!'

common noun

Simply the name of an ordinary, everyday non-specific thing or person, as opposed to proper nouns, which refer to the names of particular individuals or specific places. Common nouns include 'baby', 'cat', 'girl', 'hat', 'park', 'sofa' and 'table'.

comparison of adjectives

This is achieved in two different ways. Some adjectives form their comparative by adding -er to the positive or absolute form, as in 'braver', 'louder', 'madder', 'shorter' and 'taller'. Other adjectives form their comparative by using 'more' in conjunction with them, as in 'more beautiful', 'more realistic', 'more suitable' and 'more tactful'. Which is the correct form is largely a matter of length. One-syllable adjectives, such as 'loud', add -er, as 'louder'. Two-syllable adjectives sometimes have both forms as a possibility, as in 'gentler/more gentle', and 'cleverest/most clever'. Adjectives with three or more syllables usually form their comparatives with 'more', as in 'more comfortable', 'more gracious', 'more regular' and 'more understanding'. Some adjectives are irregular in their comparative forms, as in 'good/better', 'bad/worse', 'many/more'. Only if they begin with *un-* are they likely to end in -er, as in 'untrustworthier'.

Some adjectives by their very definitions do not normally have a comparative form, for example 'unique'.

complement

The equivalent of the OBJECT in a clause with a LINKING VERB. In the sentence 'Jack is a policeman', 'a policeman' is the complement. In the sentence 'Jane is a good mother', 'a good mother' is the complement', and in the sentence 'His son is an excellent football player', 'an excellent football player' is the complement.

complex sentence

A type of sentence in which there is a MAIN CLAUSE and one or more subordinate clauses. The sentence 'We went to visit him although he had been unfriendly to us' is a complex sentence since it is composed of a main clause and one subordinate clause ('although he had been unfriendly to us'). The sentence 'We wondered where he had gone and why he was upset' is a complex sentence since it has a main clause and two subordinate clauses ('where he had gone' and 'why he was upset').

compound sentence

A type of sentence with more than one clause and linked by a coordinating conjunction, such as 'and' or 'but', as in 'He applied for a new job and got it' and 'I went to the cinema but I didn't enjoy the film'.

concord see number agreement.

concrete noun

The name of something that one can touch, as opposed to an abstract noun, which one cannot. Concrete nouns include 'bag', 'glass', 'plate', 'pot', 'clothes', 'field', 'garden', 'flower', 'potato', 'foot' and 'shoe'. See ABSTRACT NOUN.

conjunction

A word that connects words, clauses or sentences. Conjunctions are of two types. A **coordinating conjunction** joins units of equal status, as in 'bread and butter', 'We asked for some food and we got it'. A **subordinating conjunction** joins a dependent or subordinating clause to main verbs: in 'We asked him why he was there', 'why he was there' is a subordinate clause and thus 'why' is a subordinating conjunction.

content words see function word.

continuous tenses see tense.

contraction see abbreviation.

copula *see* **linking verb**.

copular verb *see* **equative** and **linking verb**.

count noun is the same as COUNTABLE NOUN.
countable noun is one which can be preceded by 'a' and can take a plural, as in 'hat/hats', 'flower/flowers'. *See also* UNCOUNTABLE NOUN.

D

dangling participle
A participle that has been misplaced in a sentence. A participle is often used to introduce a phrase that is attached to a subject mentioned later in a sentence, as in 'Worn out by the long walk, she fell to the ground in a faint'. 'Worn out' is the participle and 'she' the subject. Another example is 'Laughing in glee at having won, she ordered some champagne'. In this sentence 'laughing' is the participle and 'she' is the subject. It is a common error for such a participle not to be related to any subject, as in 'Imprisoned in the dark basement, it seemed a long time since she had seen the sun'. This participle is said to be 'dangling'. Another example of a dangling participle is contained in 'Living alone, the days seemed long'.

It is also a common error for a participle to be related to the wrong subject in a sentence, as in 'Painting the ceiling, some of the plaster fell on his head', 'Painting' is the participle and should go with a subject 'he'. Instead it goes with 'some of the plaster'. Participles in this situation are more correctly known as **misrelated participles**, although they are also called dangling participles.

dash
A punctuation mark in the form of a short line that indicates a

short break in the continuity of a sentence, as in 'He has never been any trouble at school—quite the reverse', 'I was amazed when he turned up—I thought he was still abroad'. In such situations it serves the same purpose as brackets, except that it is frequently considered more informal. The dash should be used sparingly. Depending on it too much can lead to careless writing with ideas set down at random rather than turned into a piece of coherent prose.

The dash can be used to emphasize a word or phrase, as in 'They said goodbye then—forever'. It can also be used to add a remark to the end of a sentence, as in 'They had absolutely no money—a regular state of affairs towards the end of the month.' The dash can also be used to introduce a statement that amplifies or explains what has been said, as in 'The burglars took everything of value—her jewellery, the silver, the TV set, her hi-fi and several hundred pounds.' It can be used to summarize what has gone before, as in 'Disease, poverty, ignorance—these are the problems facing us.'

The dash is also used to introduce an afterthought, as in 'You can come with me—but you might not want to'. It can also introduce a sharp change of subject, as in 'I'm just making tea—what was that noise?' It can also be used to introduce some kind of balance in a sentence, as in 'It's going to take two of us to get this table out of here—one to move it and one to hold the door open.'

The dash is sometimes found in pairs. A pair of dashes acts in much the same way as a set of round brackets. A pair of dashes can be used to indicate a break in a sentence, as in 'We prayed—prayed as we had never prayed before—that the children would be safe', 'It was—on reflection—his best performance yet', and 'He introduced me to his wife—an attractive pleasant woman—before he left'.

Dashes are used to indicate hesitant speech, as in 'I don't— well—maybe—you could be right'. They can be used to indicate the omission of part of a word or name, as in 'It's none of your b— business', 'He's having an affair with Mrs D-'.

They can also be used between points in time or space, as in 'Edinburgh—London' and '1750—1790.'

dates

These are usually written in figures, as in 1956, rather than in words, as in nineteen fifty-six, except in formal contexts, such as legal documents. There are various ways of writing dates. The standard form in Britain is becoming day followed by month followed by year, as in '24 February 1970'. In North America the standard form of this is 'February 24, 1970', and that is a possibility in Britain also. Alternatively, some people write '24th February 1970'. Care should be taken with the writing of dates entirely in numbers, especially if one is corresponding with someone in North America. In Britain the day of the month is put first, the month second and the year third, as in '2/3/50', '2 March 1950'. In North America the month is put first, followed by the day of the month and the year. Thus in North America '2/3/50 would be 3 February 1950.

Centuries may be written either in figures, as in 'the 19th century', or in words, as in 'the nineteenth century'.

Decades and centuries are now usually written without apostrophes. as in '1980s' and '1990s'.

dative case

The case that indicates 'to' or 'for'. This is applicable to Latin but not to English, where such meanings are expressed by prepositional phrases. In English the INDIRECT OBJECT is equivalent to the dative case in some situations.

deca-
A prefix derived from Greek meaning 'ten', as in decade, decathlon and decahedron.

deci-
A prefix derived from Latin meaning 'tenth', as in decibel, decimal, decimate and decilitre.

declarative sentence
A sentence that conveys information. The subject precedes the verb in it. Examples include 'They won the battle', 'He has moved to another town', 'Lots of people go there' and 'There is a new person in charge'.

declarative mood the same as **indicative mood**.

declension
The variation of the form of a noun, adjective or pronoun to show different cases, such as nominative and accusative. It also refers to the class into which such words are placed, as in first declension, second declension, etc. The term applies to languages such as Latin but is not applicable to English.

definite article
A term for 'the', which is the most frequently used word in the English language. 'The' is used to refer back to a person or thing that has already been mentioned, as in 'Jack and Jill built a model. The model was of a ship' and 'We've bought a car. It was the cheapest car we could find'.

'The' can be used to make a general statement about all things of a particular type, as in 'The computer has led to the loss of many jobs' and 'The car has caused damage to the environment'. 'The' can be used to refer to a whole class or group, as in 'the Italians', 'the Browns' and 'the younger generation'.

'The' can also be used to refer to services or systems, as in 'They are not on the phone' and 'She prefers going by the bus'. It can be used to refer to the name of a musical instrument when someone's ability to play it is being referred to, as in 'Her son is learning to play the violin'.

'The' indicates a person or thing to be the only one, as in the Bible, the King of Spain, the White House, the Palace of Westminster and the President of the United States.

'The' can be used instead of a possessive determiner to refer to parts of the body, as in 'She took him by the arm' and 'The dog bit him on the leg'.

'The' is used in front of superlative adjectives, as in 'the largest amount of money' and 'the most beautiful woman'. It can also be used to indicate that a person or thing is unique or exceptional, as in 'the political debater of his generation'. In this last sense 'the' is pronounced 'thee'.

degree

A level of comparison of gradable adjectives. The degrees of comparison comprise **absolute** or **positive**, as in 'big', 'calm', 'dark', 'fair', 'hot', 'late', 'short' and 'tall'; **comparative**, as in 'bigger', 'calmer', 'darker', 'fairest', 'hotter', 'late', 'shorter' and 'taller'; **superlative**, as in 'biggest', 'calmest', 'darkest', 'fairest', 'hottest', 'latest', 'shortest' and 'tallest'.

Degree can also refer to adverbs. Adverbs of degree include

'extremely', 'very', 'greatly', 'rather', 'really', 'remarkably', 'terribly', as in 'an extremely rare case', 'a very old man', 'He's remarkably brave' and 'We're terribly pleased'.

demi-

A prefix derived from old French meaning 'half', as in demigod and demijohn.

demonstrative determiner

A determiner that is used to indicate things or people in relationship to the speaker or writer in space or time. 'This' and 'these' indicate nearness to the speaker, as in 'Will you take this book home?' and 'These flowers are for you'. 'That' and 'those' indicate distance from the speaker, as in 'Get that creature out of here!' and 'Aren't those flowers over there beautiful!'

demonstrative pronoun

A pronoun that is similar to a DEMONSTRATIVE DETERMINER except that it stands alone in place of a noun rather than preceding a noun, as in 'I'd like to give you this', 'What is that?', 'These are interesting books' and 'Those are not his shoes'.

dependent clause

A clause that cannot stand alone and make sense, unlike an independent or MAIN CLAUSE. Dependent clauses depend on the main clause. The term is the same as SUBORDINATE CLAUSE.

derivation

(1) The etymology of a word, as in 'The derivation of the expression is unknown'.
(2) The process of forming a new word by adding an AFFIX of

some kind to an existing word or base, as in 'helpless' from 'help' and 'maker' from 'make'.

derivative

A word that is formed by DERIVATION. For example, 'sweetly' is a derivative of 'sweet', 'peaceful' is a derivative from 'peace', 'clinging' is derived from from 'cling' and 'shortest' is derived from 'short'.

derm-

A prefix derived from Greek meaning 'skin', as in dermatitis, dermatologist and dermatology.

determiner

A word that is used in front of a noun or pronoun to tell us something about it. Unlike an ADJECTIVE, it does not, strictly speaking, 'describe' a noun or pronoun. Determiners are divided into the following categories: **articles** (a, an, the) as in 'a cat', 'an eagle', 'the book'; **demonstrative determiners** (this, that, these, those), as in 'this girl', 'that boy' and 'those people'; **possessive determiners** (my, your, his/her/its, our, their), as in 'my dog', 'her house', 'its colour', 'their responsibility'; **numbers** (one, two, three, four, etc, first, second, third, fourth, etc), as in 'two reasons', 'five ways', 'ten children'; and **indefinite** or **general determiners** (all, another, any, both, each, either, enough, every, few, fewer, less, little, many, most, much, neither, no, other, several, some), as in 'both parents', 'enough food', 'several issues'. Many words used as determiners are also pronouns. See ADJECTIVE; DEMONSTRATIVE DETERMINER; POSSESSIVE DETERMINER; NUMBERS; INDEFINITE DETERMINER.

di-

A prefix derived from Greek meaning 'two' or 'double', as in dioxide, dilemma, diphthong and disyllabic.

dia-

A prefix meaning 'through', as in diaphanous; 'apart', as in diacritical, diaphragm and dialysis; and 'across', as in diameter.

diacritic

A mark placed over, under or through a letter to indicate a sound or stress value different from that of the same letter when it is unmarked. Diacritics include the cedilla, as in 'façade', the German umlaut, as in 'mädchen', and diaeresis, as in 'naïve'.

diaeresis

A mark that is placed over a vowel to indicate that it is sounded separately from a neighbouring vowel, as in 'naïve', 'Chloë'.

dialect

A variety of language that is distinct from other varieties in terms of pronunciation, accent, vocabulary, grammar and sentence structure. The term 'dialect' tends to imply a deviation from some standard form of language, usually the dialect used by educated upper-class or upper-middle-class people, known in English as 'standard' English.

Dialects may be regional in nature. Thus in Britain there is a Cornish dialect, a Liverpool dialect, a Glasgow dialect, and so on. Alternatively, they may be based on class differences, when they are sometimes known as 'social dialects'. These include working-class dialect, upper-class dialect, and so on.

At one time regional dialects were looked down on by people who spoke only standard English. People with regional accents, using regional dialects, were unlikely to get jobs in professions such as radio and television, where the use of language was a major consideration. People intent on such careers tried to change their accents to remove all traces of dialect. However, things have changed, and now it is quite common for people using regional accents and dialects to have jobs associated with radio and television.

Note that the word 'dialect' is not appropriate if it is a global variety of English that is being referred to. For example, the English spoken in America is known as American English.

diction

(1) The choice of words in writing or speech, especially with regard to correctness, clarity or effectiveness, as in 'The content of his essay was very interesting but his diction was poor'.
(2) The pronunciation and enunciation of words in speaking and singing, as in 'She has a beautiful natural singing voice but should take lessons in diction'.

dialogue

The conversation in novels, etc, which is placed on a new line, often in a new paragraph, if there is a change of speaker, as in:

'We're going now', said John. 'Do you want to join us? If you do you'd better hurry. We can't wait.'

'Just go on', replied Mary. 'I'm not quite ready. I'll catch you up'.

digraph

A group of two letters representing one sound, as in 'ay' in 'hay', 'ey' in 'key', 'oy' in 'boy', 'ph' in 'phone' and 'th' in 'thin'. When the digraph consists of two letters physically joined together, as 'ae', it is called a 'ligature'.

diminutive

Something small or a small form or version of something, as in 'booklet', 'droplet', 'flatlet', 'auntie', 'doggy', 'islet', 'piglet', 'poppet', 'snippet', 'starlet', 'kitchenette', 'hillock', 'paddock', 'mannikin', 'lambkin', 'duckling', 'gosling', 'nestling', 'majorette', 'pipette'. Proper names often have diminutive forms, as in Alf for Alfred, Annie for Ann, Babs for Barbara, Bill for William, Charlie for Charles, Dot for Dorothy, Jimmy for James, Lizzie for Elizabeth, Meg for Margaret, Nell for Helen, Pat for Patrick and Teddy for Edward.

diphthong

A speech sound that changes its quality within the same single syllable. The sound begins as for one vowel and moves on as for another. Since the sound glides from one vowel into another, a diphthong is sometimes called a **gliding vowel**. Examples include the vowels sounds in 'rain', 'weigh', 'either', 'voice', 'height', 'aisle', 'road', 'soul', 'know', 'house', 'care', 'pure', 'during', 'here' and 'weird'.

direct object

The noun, noun phrase, noun or nominal clause or pronoun that is acted upon by the action of a transitive verb. In the sentence 'She bought milk', 'bought' is a transitive verb and 'milk' is a noun which is the direct object. In the sentence 'She bought loads of clothes', 'bought' is a transitive verb and 'loads of clothes' is the direct object. In the sentence 'He knows what happened', 'knows' is a transitive verb and 'what happened' is a 'noun clause' or 'nominal clause'. A direct object is frequently known just as object. See INDIRECT OBJECT.

direct speech

The reporting of speech by repeating exactly the actual words used by the speaker. In the sentence 'Peter said, "I am tired of this"', "I am tired of this" is a piece of direct speech because it represents exactly what Peter said. Similarly, in the sentence 'Jane asked, "Where are you going?"', "Where are you going" is a piece of direct speech since it represents exactly what Jane said.

QUOTATION MARKS are used at the beginning and end of pieces of direct speech. Only the words actually spoken are placed within the quotation marks, as in '"If I were you," he said, "I would refuse to go"'. The quotation marks involved can be either single or double, according to preference or house style.

If there is a statement such as 'he said' following the piece of direct speech, a comma is placed before the second inverted comma, as in '"Come along," he said'. If the piece of direct speech is a question or exclamation, a question mark or exclamation mark is put instead of the comma, as in '"What are you doing?" asked John' and '"Get away from me!" she screamed'.

If a statement such as 'he said' is placed within a sentence in direct speech, a comma is placed after 'he said' and the second part of the piece of direct speech does not begin with a capital letter, as in '"I know very well," he said, "that you do not like me."'

If the piece of direct speech includes a complete sentence, the sentence begins with a capital letter, as in "'I am going away," she said, "and I am not coming back. I don't feel that I belong here anymore."' Note that the full stop at the end of a piece of direct speech that is a sentence should go before the closing inverted comma.

If the piece of direct speech quoted takes up more than one paragraph, quotation marks are placed at the beginning of each new paragraph. However, quotation marks are not placed at the end of each paragraph, just at the end of the final one.

When writing a story, etc, that includes dialogue or conversation, each new piece of direct speech should begin on a new line or sometimes in a new paragraph.

Quotation marks are not used only to indicate direct speech. For example, they are sometimes used to indicate the title of a book or newspaper. The quotation marks used in this way can be either single or double, according to preference or house style. If a piece of direct speech contains the title of a book, newspaper, etc, it should be put in the opposite type of quotation marks to those used to enclose the piece of direct speech. Thus, if single quotation marks have been used in the direct speech, then double quotation marks should be used for the title within the direct speech, as in "Have you read "Animal Farm" by George Orwell?' the teacher asked'. If double quotation marks have been used for the direct speech, single quotation marks should be used for the title, as in "'Have you read 'Animal Farm?' by George Orwell?" the teacher asked'.

Sometimes titles are put in italic type instead of quotation marks. This avoids the clumsiness that can occur when both sets of quotation marks end on the same word, as in 'The pupil replied, 'No, I have not read "Animal Farm".'

dis-
A prefix derived from Latin indicating 'opposite', 'not', as in disappear, disapprove, disband, disbelieve, disclaim, disconnect, discontinue, disenchant, disengage, disinherit, dislike, disobey, dispossess, distrust and disunite.

distributive pronoun
A pronoun that refers to individual members of a class or group. These include 'each', 'either', 'neither', 'none', 'everyone', 'no one'. Such pronouns, where relevant, should be accompanied by singular verbs and singular personal pronouns, as in 'All the men are to be considered for the new posts. Each is to send in his application'. Problems arise when the sex of the noun to which the distributive pronoun refers back is either unknown or unspecified. Formerly it was the convention to treat such nouns as masculine and so to make the distributive pronoun masculine, as in 'All pupils must obey the rules. Each is to provide his own sports equipment'. Nowadays this convention is frequently considered to be unacceptably sexist and attempts have been made to get round this. One solution is to use 'him/her' (or 'him or her'), etc, as in 'The students have received a directive from the professor. Each is to produce his/her essay by tomorrow.' This convention is considered by many people to be clumsy. They prefer to be ungrammatical and use a plural personal pronoun, as in 'The pupils are being punished. Each is to inform their parents'. Where possible it is preferable to rephrase sentences to avoid

being either sexist or ungrammatical, as in 'All of the pupils must tell their parents.'

Each, either, etc, in such contexts is fairly formal. In less formal situations 'each of', 'either of', etc, is more usual, as in 'Each of the boys will have to train really hard to win' and 'Either of the dresses is perfectly suitable'.

disyllabic

A term that describes a word with two syllables. For example, 'window' is disyllabic, since it consists of the syllable 'win' and the syllable 'dow'. Similarly 'curtain' is disyllabic since it consists of the syllable 'cur' and 'tain'.

do

An auxiliary verb that is used to form negative forms, as in, 'I do not agree with you', 'They do not always win', 'He does not wish to go' and 'She did not approve of their behaviour'. It is also used to form interrogative forms, as in 'Do you agree?', 'Does she know about it?', 'Did you see that?' and 'I prefer to go by train. Don't you?' Do is also used for emphasis, as in 'I do believe you're right' and 'They do know, don't they?'

-dom

A suffix meaning 'state, condition', as in boredom, freedom, officialdom, martyrdom. It can also mean 'rank or status', as in earldom, dukedom, or 'domain, territory' as in kingdom.

double negative

The occurrence of two negative words in a single sentence or clause, as in 'He didn't say nothing' and 'We never had no quarrel'. This is usually considered incorrect in standard English, although it is a feature of some social or regional dialects. The use of the double negative, if taken literally, often has the opposite meaning to the one intended. Thus 'He didn't say nothing' conveys the idea that 'He said something'.

Some double negatives are considered acceptable, as in 'I wouldn't be surprised if they don't turn up', although it is better to restrict such constructions to informal contexts. The sentence quoted conveys the impression that the speaker will be quite surprised if 'they' do 'turn up'. Another example of an acceptable double negative is 'I can't not worry about the children. Anything could have happened to them'. Again this type of construction is best restricted to informal contexts.

It is the semi-negative forms, such as 'hardly' and 'scarcely', that cause most problems with regard to double negatives, as in 'We didn't have hardly any money to buy food' and 'They didn't have barely enough time to catch the bus'. Such sentences are incorrect.

double passive

A clause that contains two verbs in the passive, the second of which is an infinitive, as in 'The goods are expected to be despatched some time this week'. Some examples of double passives are clumsy or ungrammatical and should be avoided, as in 'Redundancy notices are proposed to be issued next week'.

doubling of consonants

These can cause spelling problems. There are a few rules that help to solve these problems. These include the following: In words of one syllable ending in a single consonant preceded by a single vowel, the consonant is doubled when an ending starting with a vowel is added, as in 'drop' and 'dropped', 'pat' and 'patting' and 'rub' and 'rubbing'.

In words of more than one syllable that end in a single consonant preceded by a single vowel, the consonant is doubled if the stress is on the last syllable, as in 'begin' and 'beginning', 'occur' and 'occurring', 'prefer' and 'preferred', 'refer' and 'referring' and 'commit' and 'committed'. In similar words where the stress is not on the last syllable, the consonant does not double, as in 'bigot' and 'bigoted' and 'develop' and 'developed'.

Exceptions to this rule include words ending in 'l'. The 'l' doubles even in cases where the last syllable containing it is unstressed, as in 'travel' and 'travelled' and 'appal' and 'appalling'. 'Worship', in which the stress is on the first syllable, is also an exception, as in 'worshipped'.

doubles

Words that habitually go together, as in 'out and out', 'neck and neck', 'over and over', 'hale and hearty', 'rant and rave', 'fast and furious', 'hue and cry', 'stuff and nonsense', 'rough and ready', 'might and main', 'give and take', 'ups and downs', 'fair and square', 'high and dry' and 'wear and tear'. Doubles are also sometimes called **dyads**.

doublets

Pairs of words that have developed from the same original word but now differ somewhat in form and usually in meaning. Examples include 'human' and 'humane', 'shade' and 'shadow', 'hostel' and 'hotel', 'frail' and 'fragile', and 'fashion' and 'faction'.

dramatic irony

A situation in which a character in a play, novel, etc, says or does something that has a meaning for the audience or reader, other than the obvious meaning, that he/she does not understand. Its use is common in both comedy and tragedy.

dual gender

A category of nouns in which there is no indication of gender. The nouns referred to include a range of words used for people, and occasionally animals, which can be of either gender. Unless the gender is specified we do not know the sex of the person referred to. Such words include 'artist', 'author', 'poet', 'singer', 'child', 'pupil', 'student', 'baby', 'parent', 'teacher', 'dog'. Such words give rise to problems with accompanying singular pronouns. See EACH.

dummy subject

A SUBJECT that has no intrinsic meaning but is inserted to maintain a balanced grammatical structure. In the sentences 'It has started to rain' and 'It is nearly midnight', 'it' is a dummy subject. In the sentences 'There is nothing else to say' and 'There is no reason for his behaviour', 'there' is a dummy subject.

dyads see doubles.

dynamic verb

A verb with a meaning that indicates action, as 'work' in 'They work hard', 'play' in 'The boys play football at the weekend' and 'come' in 'The girls come here every Sunday'.

dys-

A prefix derived from the Greek meaning 'bad', as in dyslexia, dysgraphia, dysmenorrhea, dyspepsia.

E

each

A word that can be either a DETERMINER or a DISTRIBUTIVE PRO-
NOUN. Each as a determiner is used before a singular noun and
is accompanied by a singular verb, as in 'Each candidate is to
reapply', 'Each athlete has a place in the final', 'Each country is
represented by a head of state' and 'Each chair was covered in
chintz'.

   Each of can sometimes be used instead of each, as in 'each
of the candidates'. Again a singular verb is used, as in 'Each of
the books has pages missing', 'Each of the chairs has a broken
leg' and 'Each of the pupils is to make a contribution to the
cost of the outing'. Each of can also be used in front of plural
pronouns, as in 'each of them'. Once again a singular verb is
used, as in 'Each of them wants something different', 'Each of
us is supposed to make a contribution' and 'Each of the words
has several meanings'. If the user wishes to emphasize the fact
that something is true about every member of a group, **each
one of** should be used and not 'every', as in 'Each one of them
feels guilty', 'Each one of us has a part to play' and 'Each one of
the actors has improved'.

   As a pronoun, each also takes a singular verb, as in 'They hate
each other. Each is plotting revenge', 'These exercises are not
a waste of time. Each provides valuable experience'. For emphasis **each one** can be used, as in 'We cannot leave any of

these books behind. Each one of them is necessary' and 'We should not dismiss any of the staff. Each one has a part to play in the new firm'.

Each, where relevant, should be accompanied by a singular personal pronoun, as in 'Each girl has to provide her own sports equipment', 'Each of the men is to take a turn at working night shift', 'The boys are all well off and each can afford the cost of the holiday' and 'There are to be no exceptions among the women staff. Each one has to work full time'.

Problems arise when the noun that each refers back to is of unknown or unspecified sex. Formerly nouns in such situations were assumed to be masculine, as in 'Each pupil was required to bring his own tennis racket' and 'Each of the students has to provide himself with a tape recorder'. Nowadays such a convention is regarded as being sexist and the use of 'he/her', 'his/her', etc, is proposed, as in 'Each pupil was required to bring his/her (or 'his or her') own tennis racket' and 'Each student has to provide himself/herself (or 'himself or herself') with a tape recorder'. Even in written English such a convention can be clumsy and it is even more so in spoken English. For this reason many people decide to be ungrammatical and opt for 'Each pupil was required to bring their own tennis racket' and 'Each student has to provide themselves with a tape recorder'.

Both sexism and grammatical error can be avoided by re-phrasing such sentences, as in 'All pupils are required to bring their own tennis rackets' and 'All students have to provide themselves with tape recorders'.

Each is used rather than every when the user is thinking of the members of a group as individuals.

eco-

A prefix indicating ecology. Following the increased awareness of the importance of the environment, there has been a growing interest in ecology and many words beginning with eco-have been added to the English language. Some of these are scientific terms such as ecotype, ecosystem or ecospecies. Others are more general terms, such as ecocatastrophe and ecopolitics, and some are even slang terms, such as ecofreak and econut.

-ectomy

A suffix of Greek origin that indicates 'surgical removal', as in hysterectomy (the surgical removal of the womb), mastectomy (the surgical removal of a breast) and appendicectomy (the surgical removal of the appendix, the American English version of which is appendectomy).

-ed

A suffix that forms the past tense and past participles of regular verbs, as in 'asked', 'blinded', 'caused', 'darkened', 'escaped', 'frightened', 'guarded', 'hunted', 'injured', 'jilted', 'kicked', 'landed', 'marked', 'noted', 'opened', 'painted', 'quarrelled', 'rattled', 'started', 'tormented', 'unveiled', 'washed', 'yielded'. Some past participles ending in '-ed' can act as adjectives, as in 'darkened room', 'escaped prisoners', 'frightened children', 'hunted animals', 'painted faces' and 'tormented souls'.

In the case of some verbs, the past tense and past participle may end in '-ed' or 't', according to preference. Such verbs include 'burn', 'dream', 'dwell', 'kneel', 'lean', 'leapt', 'smell', 'spell', 'spill' and 'spoil'. Thus 'burned' and 'burnt', 'dreamed' and 'dreamt', 'kneeled' and 'knelt', and 'learned' and 'learnt', etc, are acceptable forms.

-ee

A suffix that is derived from French and is used as part of nouns that are the recipients of an action, as in deportee (a person who has been deported); employee (a person who is employed); interviewee (a person who is being interviewed); licensee (a person who has been licensed); trainee (a person who is being trained).

  -Ee can also be used as part of a noun indicating a person who acts or behaves in a particular way, as absentee (a person who absents himself/herself) and escapee (a person who escapes).

e.g.

The abbreviation of the Latin phrase *exempli gratia*, which means 'for example'. It is used before examples of what has previously been referred to, as in 'The tourists want to visit the historic sites of Edinburgh, e.g. Edinburgh Castle and Holyrood House'. By its very nature e.g. is mostly restricted to written English, becoming 'for example' in speech. Many writers also prefer to use 'for example' rather than use e.g. Both letters of the abbreviation usually have a full stop after them, as e.g., and it is usually preceded by a comma.

either

A word that can be used as either a determiner or distributive pronoun. As a determiner it is used with a singular verb, as in 'Either hotel is expensive' and 'In principle they are both against the plan but is either likely to vote for it?'

Either of can be used instead of either. It is used before a plural noun, as in 'either of the applicants' and 'either of the houses'. It is accompanied by a singular verb, as in 'Either of the applicants is suitable' and 'Either of the houses is big enough for their family'.

Either can be used as a distributive pronoun and takes a singular verb, as in 'We have looked at both houses and either is suitable' and 'She cannot decide between the two dresses but either is appropriate for the occasion'. This use is rather formal.

In the **either .... or** construction, a singular verb is used if both subjects are singular, as in 'Either Mary or Jane knows what to do' and 'Either my mother or my father plans to be present'. A plural verb is used if both nouns involved are plural, as in 'Either men or women can play' and 'Either houses or flats are available'.

When a combination of singular and plural subjects is involved, the verb traditionally agrees with the subject that is nearer to it, as in 'Either his parents or his sister is going to come' and 'Either his grandmother or his parents are going to come'.

As a pronoun, either should be used only of two possibilities.

electro-
A prefix meaning 'electric, electrical' as in electrocardiograph, electromagnetic, electroscope, electrotherapy.

elision
The omission of a speech sound or syllable, as in the omission

of 'd' in one of the possible pronunciations of 'Wednesday' and in the omission of 'ce' from the pronunciation of 'Gloucester'.

ellipsis

An omission of some kind. It can refer to the omission of words from a statement because they are thought to be obvious from the context. In many cases it involves using an auxiliary verb on its own rather than a full verb, as in 'Jane won't accept it but Mary will' and 'They would go if they could'. In such cases the full form of 'Jane won't accept it but Mary will accept it' and 'They would go if they could go' would sound unnatural and repetitive. This is common in spoken English.

Some sentences containing an ellipsis sound clumsy as well as ungrammatical, as in 'This is as good, or perhaps even better than that', where 'as' is omitted after 'good' and in 'People have and still do express their disapproval about it', where 'expressed' is omitted after 'have'. Care should be taken to avoid ellipsis if the use of it is going to be ambiguous or clumsy.

Ellipsis is often used to indicate an omission from a quoted passage. If part of a passage is quoted and there is a gap before the next piece of the same passage is required to be quoted, an ellipsis is used in the form of three dots (. . .). If the part of the passage quoted does not start at the beginning of a sentence the ellipsis precedes it.

emphasizing adjective

An adjective that is used for emphasis. 'Very' is an emphasizing adjective in the sentence 'His very mother dislikes him' and 'own' is an emphasizing adjective in 'He likes to think that he is his own master'.

emphasizing adverb

An adverb used for emphasis. 'Really' is an emphasizing adverb in the sentence 'She really doesn't care whether she lives or dies', and 'positively' is an emphasizing adverb in the sentence 'He positively does not want to know anything about it'.

emphatic pronoun

A reflexive pronoun that is used for emphasis, as in 'He knows himself that he is wrong', 'She admitted herself that she had made a mistake' and 'The teachers themselves say that the headmaster is too strict'.

-en

A suffix with several functions. In one sense it indicates 'causing to be', as in broaden, darken, gladden, lighten and sweeten. It also indicates a diminutive or small version of something, as in chicken and maiden. It also indicates what something is made of, as in silken, wooden and woollen. It is also used to form the past participle of many irregular verbs, such as 'broken', 'fallen', 'forgotten' and 'taken'.

en-

A prefix indicating 'causing to be', as in enrich and enlarge, and 'putting into', as in endanger, enrage, enslave.

ending

The final part of a word consisting of an inflection that is added to a BASE or root word. The '-ren' part of 'children' is an ending, the '-er' of 'poorer' is an ending and the '-ing' of 'falling' is an ending.

epic

A word that originally referred to a very long narrative poem dealing with heroic deeds and adventures on a grand scale, as Homer's *Iliad*. In modern usage it has been extended to include novels or films with some of these qualities.

epigram

A figure of speech consisting of a brief, pointed and witty saying, as in Jonathan Swift's 'Every man desires to live long; but no man would be old' and Oscar Wilde's 'A cynic is a man who knows the price of everything and the value of nothing'. 'Epigram' originally referred to a short poem inscribed on a public monument or tomb.

epithet

An adjective that describes a quality of a noun, as in 'a beautiful dress', 'an amazing story' and 'an enjoyable occasion'. It is also used to indicate a term of abuse, as in 'The drunk man let out a stream of epithets at the policeman.'

eponym

A person after whom something is named. The name of the thing in question can also be referred to as an eponym, or it can be said to be **eponymous**, eponymous being the adjective from eponym. English has several eponymous words. Some of these are listed below together with their derivations:

Bailey bridge, a type of temporary military bridge that can be assembled very quickly, called after Sir Donald **Bailey** (1901-85), the English engineer who invented it.

Bowie knife, a type of hunting knife with a long curving blade, called after the American soldier and adventurer, James **Bowie** (1799-1836), who made it popular.

cardigan, a knitted jacket fastened with buttons called after the Earl of **Cardigan** (1797-1868) who was fond of wearing such a garment and was the British cavalry officer who led the unsuccessful Charge of the Light Brigade during the Crimean War (1854).

Celsius the temperature scale, called after the Swedish astronomer, Anders **Celsius** (1701-44).

freesia, a type of sweet-smelling flower, called after the German physician, Friedrich Heinrich Theodor **Freese** (died 1876).

garibaldi, a type of biscuit with a layer of currants in it, called after Giuseppe **Garibaldi** (1807-1882), an Italian soldier patriot who is said to have enjoyed such biscuits.

Granny Smith, a variety of hard green apple, called after the Australian gardener, Maria Ann Smith, known as **Granny Smith** (died 1870), who first grew the apple in Sydney in the 1860s.

greengage, a type of greenish plum, called after Sir William **Gage** who introduced it into Britain from France (1777-1864).

leotard, a one-piece, close-fitting garment worn by acrobats and dancers, called after the French acrobat, Jules **Leotard** (1842-70), who introduced the costume as a circus garment.

mackintosh, a type of raincoat, especially one made of rubberized cloth, called after the Scottish chemist, Charles **Mackintosh** (1766-1843), who patented it in the early 1820s.

praline, a type of confectionery made from nuts and sugar, is called after Count Plessis-**Praslin** (1598-1675), a French field marshal, whose chef is said to have been the first person to make the sweet.

plimsoll, a type of light rubber-soled canvas shoe, called after the English shipping reform leader, Samuel **Plimsoll** (1824-98). The shoe is so named because the upper edge of the rubber was thought to resemble the **Plimsoll** Line, the set of markings on the side of a ship which indicate the levels to which the ship may be safely loaded. The Plimsoll Line became law in 1876.

salmonella, the bacteria that causes some diseases such as food poisoning, called after Daniel Elmer **Salmon** (1850-1914), the American veterinary surgeon who identified it.

sandwich, a snack consisting of two pieces of buttered bread with a filling, called after the Earl of **Sandwich** (1718-92) who was such a compulsive gambler that he would not leave the gaming tables to eat, but had some cold beef between two slices of bread brought to him.

saxophone, a type of keyed brass instrument often used in jazz music, called after Adolphe **Sax** (1814-94), the Belgium instrument-maker who invented it.

shrapnel, an explosive projectile that contains bullets or fragments of metal and a charge that is exploded before impact, called after the British army officer, Henry **Shrapnel** (1761-1842), who invented it.

stetson, a type of wide-brimmed, high-crowned felt hat, called after its designer, the American hat-maker, John Batterson **Stetson** (1830-1906).

trilby, a type of soft felt hat with an indented crown, called after 'Trilby', the dramatized version of the novel by the English writer, George du Maurier. The heroine of the play, Trilby O'Ferrall, wore such a hat.

wellington, a waterproof rubber boot that extends to the knee, called after the Duke of **Wellington** (1769-1852), who defeated Napoleon at Waterloo (1815).

equative

A term that indicates that one thing is equal to, or the same as, another. The verb 'to be' is sometimes known as an **equative verb** because it links a subject and complement that are equal to each other, as in 'He is a rogue' ('he' and 'rogue' refer to the same person) and 'His wife is a journalist' ('his wife' and 'journalist' refer to the same person). Other equative verbs include 'appear', 'become', 'look', 'remain' and 'seem', as in 'She looks a nasty person' and 'He became a rich man'. Such verbs are more usually known as **copular verbs**.

-er

A suffix with several functions. It can indicate 'a person who does something', as in bearer, cleaner, employer, farmer, manager. Some words in this category can also end in '-or', as in adviser/advisor. It can also indicate 'a person who is engaged in something', as in lawyer. It also indicates 'a thing that does something', as in blender, cooker, mower, printer and strainer. It can also indicate the comparative form of an adjective, as in darker, fairer, older, shorter and younger. It can also indicate 'someone that comes from somewhere', as in Londoner.

-esque

A suffix of French origin that means 'in the style or fashion of', as in Junoesque, statuesque, Picassoesque, Ramboesque.

-ese

A suffix that indicates 'belonging to, coming from' and is used of people and languages, as Chinese, Japanese and Portuguese. By extension it refers to words indicating some kind of jargon, as computerese, journalese and officialese.

Esq.

A word that can be used instead of 'Mr' when addressing an envelope to a man, as in 'John Jones, Esq.'. It is mostly used in formal contexts. Note that Esq. is used instead of 'Mr', not as well as it. It is usually spelt with a full stop.

-ess

A suffix that was formerly widely used to indicate the feminine form of a word, as authoress from 'author', poetess from 'poet', editress from 'editor', and sculptress from 'sculptor'. In many cases the supposed male form, such as 'author', is now considered a neutral form and so is used of both a woman and a man. Thus a woman as well as a man may be an author, a poet, an editor and a sculptor, etc. Some words ending in -ess remain, as princess, duchess, heiress and hostess. Actress and waitress are still also fairly widespread.

-est

A suffix that indicates the superlative forms of adjectives, as in biggest, hardest, lowest, smallest, ugliest.

etc

The abbreviation of a Latin phrase et cetera, meaning 'and the rest, and other things'. It is used at the end of lists to indicate that there exist other examples of the kind of thing that has just been named, as in 'He grows potatoes, carrots, turnips, etc', 'The girls can play tennis, hockey, squash, etc', 'The main branch of the bank can supply francs, marks, lire, kroner, etc'. Etc is preceded by a comma and is also spelt with a full stop.

-ette
A suffix indicating a diminutive or smaller version, as cigarette, kitchenette, rosette, serviette. It can also indicate 'imitation', as in flannelette, leatherette, satinette. It can also indicate 'female', as in majorette, usherette, suffragette. In this last sense it is sometimes used disparagingly, as in jockette (a derogatory word for a female jockey) and hackette (a derogatory word for a female journalist).

etymology
The source of the formation of a word and the development of its meaning, as in 'What is the etymology of the word "biochemistry"?' It also means the branch of language studies that deals with the origin and development of words, as in 'He specializes in etymology'. In addition it refers to an account or statement of the formation of a word or phrase, as in 'Does that dictionary have etymologies?' In larger dictionaries it is usual to include etymologies, often at the end of each entry. These indicate which language the relevant word has been derived from, for example, whether it has come from Old English, Norse, Latin, Greek, French, German, Dutch, Italian, Spanish, etc. Alternatively they indicate which person, place, etc, the word has been named after. Some dictionaries also include the date at which the relevant word entered the English language. *See* BORROWING.

Many words and phrases in the English language are of unknown or uncertain origin. In such cases much guesswork
goes on and various suggestions put forward, most of which
cannot be proved.

euphemism
A term given to an expression that is a milder, more pleasant,
less direct way of saying something that might be thought to
be too harsh or direct. English has a great many euphemisms,
many of these referring to certain areas of life. Euphemisms
range from the high-flown, to the coy, to slang. Some examples of euphemisms and of the areas in which they tend to occur are listed below:

euphemisms for 'die' or 'be dead': be in the arms of Jesus,
be laid to rest, be with one's maker, be no longer with us, be
with the Lord, be written out of the script, bite the dust,
cash in one's chips, croak, depart this life, go to a better
place, go the way of all flesh, go to one's long home, go to the
happy hunting grounds, have been taken by the grim reaper,
have bought it, have breathed one's last, have gone to a better place, kick the bucket, meet one's end, pass away, pay the
supreme sacrifice, pop off, push up the daisies, rest in peace,
shuffle off this mortal coil, slip one's rope, turn up one's toes.

euphemisms for 'old': getting on a bit, not as young as one
was, not in the first flush of youth, in the sunset years, in the
twilight years, of advanced years, so many years young (as in
'90 years young').

euphemisms for 'suicide': do away with oneself, die by
one's own hand, end it all, make away with oneself, take one's
own life, take the easy way out, top oneself.

euphemisms for 'to dismiss': declare (someone) redundant, deselect, dispense with (someone's) services, give early retirement to, give (someone) a golden handshake, give (someone) his/her marching orders, let (someone) go, not to renew (someone's) contract.

euphemisms for 'drunk': blotto, feeling no pain, happy, half-cut, legless, merry, one over the eight, plastered, three sheets to the wind, tiddly, tipsy, tired and emotional, squiffy, well-oiled.

euphemisms for 'naked': in a state of nature, in one's birthday suit, in the buff, in the nuddy, in the raw, starkers, without a stitch, wearing only a smile.

euphemisms for 'pregnant': awaiting the patter of tiny feet, expecting, expecting a happy event, in a delicate condition, in an interesting condition, in the club, in the family way, in the pudding club, up the pole, up the spout, with a bun in the oven.

euphemisms for 'to have sexual intercourse': be intimate with, do it, get one's end away, go to bed with, have it off with, make love, make out, sleep with, score.

euphemisms for 'sexual intercourse': hanky panky, intimacy, nookie, roll in the hay, rumpy pumpy/rumpty pumpty.

euphemisms for 'to go to the toilet': answer the call of nature, freshen up, go somewhere, pay a visit, powder one's nose, spend a penny, take a slash, wash one's hands.

euphemisms for 'toilet': bathroom, bog, can, john, karzy, powder room, rest room, the facilities, the conveniences, the geography of the house, the little boys' room/the little girls' room, the littlest room, the smallest room, the plumbing, wash room.

euphemisms and political correctness: Many of the expressions advocated by the politically correct movement for viewing physical and mental disabilities in a more positive light are in fact euphemisms. These include 'aurally challenged' for 'deaf', 'optically challenged' for 'blind', and 'uniquely abled' for 'physically disabled'.

Euro-

A prefix meaning either 'referring to Europe', as in 'Eurovision', but more commonly now 'referring to the European Community', as in Euro-MP, Eurocrat, Eurocurrency.

every

A word used with a singular noun to indicate that all the members of a group are being referred to. It takes a singular verb, as in 'Every soldier must report for duty', 'Every machine is to be inspected' and 'Every house has a different view'. Every should also be accompanied, where relevant, by a singular pronoun, as in 'Every boy has his job to do', 'Every girl is to wear a dress' and 'Every machine is to be replaced'. Problems arise when the sex of the noun to which every refers is unknown or unspecified. Formerly it was the custom to assume such a noun to be masculine and to use masculine pronouns, as in 'Every pupil is to behave himself properly. This assumption is now regarded as sexist, and to avoid this 'he/she', 'him/her' and 'his/her' can be used. Many people feel that this convention can become clumsy and prefer to be ungrammatical by using 'they', 'them' and 'their', as in 'Every pupil is to behave themselves properly.' Many sentences of this kind can be rephrased to avoid being either sexist or ungrammatical, as in 'All pupils are to behave themselves properly'. See EACH.

everyone

A pronoun that takes a singular verb, as in 'Everyone is welcome' and 'Everyone has the right to a decent standard of living'. In order to be grammatically correct, it should be accompanied, where relevant, by a singular personal pronoun but it is subject to the same kind of treatment as EVERY.

ex-

A prefix meaning 'former', as in ex-chairman, ex-president, ex-wife.

exclamation

A word, phrase or sentence called out with strong feeling of some kind. It is marked by an **exclamation mark** which occurs at the end of the exclamation, as in 'Get lost!', 'What a nerve!', 'Help!', 'Ouch!' 'Well I never!', 'What a disaster!', 'I'm tired of all this!' and 'Let me out of here!' An **exclamatory question** is a sentence that is interrogative in form but is an exclamation in meaning, as in 'Isn't the baby beautiful!' and 'Isn't it lovely!'.

extra-

A prefix meaning 'beyond, outside' as in extra-marital, extra-terrestrial, extra-curricular.

F

fable

A story that is intended to convey a moral lesson. Fables frequently feature animals that speak and act like human beings. Most famous are those of Aesop, a Phrygian slave (620-560 BC), who wrote such fables as 'The Hare and the Tortoise' and 'The Fox and the Grapes'.

false friends

A term for words that have the same or similar forms in different languages but have different meanings in each. For example, the French word *abusif* and the English word 'abusive' are false friends. *Abusif* does not mean 'abusive' but 'incorrect, illegal, unauthorized, excessive'. Similarly, the French word *actuel* and the English 'actual' are false friends. *Actuel* does not mean 'actual' but 'present-day'. Similarly, the French *eventuel* and Italian *eventuale* are false friends with the English 'eventual'. *Eventuel* and *eventuale* do not mean 'eventual' but 'possible', while *sensible* in French and *sensibile* in Italian do not mean 'sensible, having good sense or judgement' but 'sensitive, tender, touchy'.

feminine

The term for the GENDER that indicates female persons or animals. It is the opposite of 'masculine'. The feminine gender demands the use of the appropriate pronoun, including 'she', 'her', 'hers' and 'herself', as in 'The girl tried to save the dog but *she* was unable to do so', 'The woman hurt *her* leg', 'Mary said that the book is *hers*', and 'The waitress cut *herself*'.

The feminine forms of words, formed by adding —*ess*, used to be common but many such forms are now thought to be sexist. Words such as 'author', 'sculptor', 'poet' are now considered to be neutral terms that can be used to refer to a man or a woman. Some -*ess* words are either still being used or are in a state of flux, as in 'actress'. See -ESS.

few and a few

These are not interchangeable. Both expressions mean 'some, but not many', but they convey different impressions. **Few** is the opposite of 'many', as in 'We have few resources' and 'We have few ideas left'. **A few** conveys a more positive impression and is the opposite of 'none', as in 'We have a few pounds set aside for Christmas' and 'We have not reached a definite decision but we have a few ideas in hand'. The sentence 'We have few ideas left' indicates a negative situation, that 'we' are running out of 'ideas', but the sentence 'We have a few ideas in hand' conveys a positive impression.

fewer and less

These are liable to be used wrongly. **Fewer** means 'a smaller number of' and should be used with plural nouns, as in 'fewer problems', 'fewer resources', 'fewer fears', 'fewer boxes', 'fewer books', 'fewer bottles' and 'fewer chairs'. **Less** means 'a smaller amount of' and should be used with singular nouns, as in 'less responsibility', less anxiety', less work', 'less milk', 'less wood' and 'less material'. It is a very common error to use less where fewer is correct, as in 'less bottles' and 'less queues'.

figurative

A term that refers to words that are not used literally. For example, 'mine' in the sense of 'excavation in the earth from which coal, tin, etc, is taken' is a literal use of the word. 'Mine' in the sense of 'He is a mine of information' is a figurative use of the word. There are many figurative expressions in English. These include 'take the bull by the horns', 'put one's shoulder to the wheel', 'hide one's light under a bushel', 'be in seventh heaven', 'count one's chickens', 'change horses in mid-stream', 'blow hot and cold', 'run with the hare and hunt with the hounds', 'make the feathers fly', 'put the cat among the pigeons', 'cut corners', 'cry over spilt milk', 'jump on the bandwagon', 'let the grass grow under one's feet', 'drop a brick', 'burn the midnight oil', 'show a clean pair of heels', 'turn one's coat', 'drive a coach and horses through' and 'take coals to Newcastle'.

figure of speech

A form of expression used to heighten the effect of a statement. The most commonly known are SIMILES and METAPHORS, but there are many more, such as PERSONIFICATION. See individual entries for further information.

finite clause

A clause that contains a FINITE VERB, as in 'when she sees him', 'after she had defeated him', and 'as they were sitting there'.

finite verb
A verb that has a tense and has a subject with which it agrees in number and person. For example 'cries' is finite in the sentence 'The child cries most of the time', and 'looks' is finite in the sentence 'The old man looks ill'. However 'go' in the sentence 'He wants to go' is non-finite since it has no variation of tense and does not have a subject. Similarly in the sentence 'Sitting on the river-bank, he was lost in thought', 'sitting' is non-finite.

first person
This refers to the person who is speaking or writing when referring to himself or herself. The **first person pronouns** are 'I', 'me', 'myself' and 'mine', with the plural forms being 'we', 'us', 'ourselves' and 'ours'. Examples include 'She said, "*I* am going home"', '"*I* am going shopping," he said', '"*We* have very little money left," she said to her husband' and 'He said, "*We* shall have to leave now if we are to get there on time"'. The **first person determiners** are 'my' and 'our', as in 'I have forgotten to bring *my* notebook' and 'We must remember to bring *our* books home.'

fixed phrase, also called **set phrase**
A phrase that has no, or virtually no, variants, as in 'from bad to worse', 'to and fro', 'hither and thither', 'horse and cart', 'this and that', 'alas and alack' and 'rough and ready'.

-fold
A suffix meaning 'times, multiplied by', as in fourfold, a hundredfold.

for-

A prefix derived from Old English with several meanings. These include 'prohibition', as in forbid; 'abstention' as in forbear, forgo and forswear; 'neglect', as in forsake; 'excess, intensity', as in forlorn; and 'away, off, apart', as in forgive.

fore-

A prefix derived from Old English meaning 'before', as in forecast, forestall, foretell, forewarn, foregoing and forefathers. It can also mean 'front', as in foreleg, forehead, forepart.

foreign plural

A plural of a word in English that has retained the plural form of the foreign word from which the English word has been derived. Examples include 'phenomena' from 'phenomenon', 'crises' from 'crisis' and 'criteria' from 'criterion'. There is a modern tendency to anglicize some of the foreign plural forms. In some cases the foreign plural form and the anglicized form exist alongside each other as 'formulae/formulas', 'thesauri/thesauruses', 'radii/radiuses', 'indices/indexes' and 'bureaux/bureaus'.

foreign expression

An expression that has been adopted into English but not 'naturalized' and is sometimes written in italic type, as in *bête noire* (a fear or obsession), *rara avis* (a rarity), *en passant* (in passing), *hors de combat*, (out of the contest, disabled), *en route* (on the way), *bon mot* (witty saying), *in toto* (completely), *in flagrante delicto* (in the very act of committing an offence), *enfant terrible* (a person who causes embarrassment by indiscreet or outrageous behaviour), *en famille* (with one's family) and *inter alia* (among other things).

-form
A suffix meaning 'having the form of', as in cruciform, or 'having such a number of', as in uniform, multiform.

formal
The term used to refer to speech and writing that is characterized by more complicated and more difficult language and by more complicated grammatical structures. Short forms and contractions are avoided in formal speech and writing. *See* IN-FORMAL.

formula
A set phrase that is used in certain conventions, as in 'How do you do?', 'Yours faithfully', 'Yours sincerely', 'Kind regards', 'See you later', 'Nice to see you!' and 'Many happy returns'.

form word *see* **function word**.

fragmentary sentence *see* **major sentence**.

-free
A suffix used to form adjectives indicating 'absence of, freedom from', as in carefree, trouble-free, anxiety-free, tax-free, duty-free, additive-free, lead-free.

-friendly
A modern suffix formed on analogy with 'user-friendly' to

mean 'helpful to, supporting', as in child-friendly, environment-friendly and ozone-friendly.

frequentative

A term referring to a verb that expresses frequent repetition of an action. In English the verb endings -le and -el sometimes indicate the frequentative form, as in 'waddle' from 'wade', 'sparkle' from 'spark', 'crackle' from 'crack' and 'dazzle' from 'daze'. The ending -er can also indicate the frequentative form, as in 'stutter', 'spatter' and 'batter'.

-ful

A suffix indicating 'the amount that fills something', as in bucketful, basinful, handful, spoonful, bagful and pocketful. It can also mean 'full of', as in beautiful, truthful and scornful. It can also mean 'having the qualities of', as in masterful, and 'apt to, able to', as in forgetful, mournful and useful.

full stop

A punctuation mark consisting of a small dot (.). Its principal use is to end a sentence that is not a question or an exclamation, as in 'They spent the money.', 'She is studying hard.', 'He has been declared redundant and is very upset.' and 'Because she is shy, she rarely goes to parties.'

The full stop is also used in decimal fractions, as in '4.5 metres', '6.3 miles' and '12.2 litres'. It can also be used in dates, as in '22.2.94', and in times, as in '3.15 tomorrow afternoon'.

In modern usage the tendency is to omit full stops from abbreviations. This is most true of abbreviations involving initial capital letters as in TUC, BBC, EEC and USA. In such cases full stops should definitely not be used if one or some of the initial letters do not belong to a full word. Thus, television is abbreviated to TV and educationally subnormal to ESN.

There are usually no full stops in abbreviations involving the first and letters of a word (contractions) Dr, Mr, Rd, St, but this is a matter of taste.

Abbreviations involving the first few letters of a word, as in 'Prof' (Professor) are the most likely to have full stops, as in 'Feb.' (February), but again this is now a matter of taste.

For the use of the full stop in direct speech see DIRECT SPEECH. The full stop can also be called **point** or **period**.

function word

A word that has very little meaning but is primarily of grammatical significance and merely performs a 'function' in a sentence. Function words include determiners, and prepositions such as in, on and up. Words that are not function words are sometimes known as **content words**.

Function word is also known as **form word** or **structure word**.

future perfect tense

The TENSE of a verb that is formed by 'will' or 'shall' together with the perfect tense, as in 'They will have been married ten years next week', 'You will have finished work by this time tomorrow' and 'By the time Jane arrives here she will have been travelling non-stop for forty-eight hours'.

future tense

The TENSE of a verb that describes actions or states that will occur at some future time. It is marked by 'will' and 'shall'. Traditionally 'shall' was used with subjects in the first person, as in 'I shall see you tomorrow' and 'We shall go there next week', and 'will' was used with subjects in the second and third person, as in 'You will find out next week', 'He will recognize her when he sees her' and 'They will be on the next train'. Formerly 'will' was used with the first person and 'shall' with the second and third person to indicate emphasis or insistence, as in 'I *will* go on my own' and 'We *will* be able to afford it'; 'You *shall* pay what you owe' and 'The children *shall* get a holiday'. In modern usage 'shall' is usually used only for emphasis or insistence, whether with the first, second or third person, except in formal contexts. Otherwise 'will' is used, as in 'I will go tomorrow', 'We will have to see', 'You will be surprised', and 'They will be on their way by now'.

The future tense can also be marked by 'be about to' plus the infinitive of the relevant verb or 'be going to' plus the infinitive of the relevant verb. Examples include 'We are about to leave for work', 'They are about to go on holiday', 'She is going to be late' and 'They are going to demolish the building'.

G

-gate

A modern suffix that is added to a noun to indicate something scandalous. Most of the words so formed are short-lived and forgotten about almost as soon as they are invented. In modern usage they are frequently used to apply to sexual scandals, but originally -gate was restricted to some form of political scandal. The suffix is derived from Watergate, and refers to a political scandal in the United States during President Richard Nixon's re-election campaign in 1972, when Republican agents were caught breaking into the headquarters of the Democratic Party in Washington, which were in a building called the Watergate Building. The uncovering of the attempts to cover up the break-in led to Richard Nixon's resignation.

gemination

The doubling of consonants before a suffix. See DOUBLING OF CONSONANTS.

gender

In the English language this usually refers to the natural distinctions of sex (or absence of sex) that exist, and nouns are classified according to these distinctions—masculine, feminine and neuter. Thus, 'man', 'boy', 'king', 'prince', 'emperor', 'duke', 'heir', 'son', 'brother', 'father', 'nephew', 'husband', 'bridegroom', 'widower', 'hero', 'cock', 'drake', 'fox' and 'lion' are masculine nouns. Similarly, 'girl', 'woman', 'queen', 'princess', 'empress', 'duchess', 'heiress', 'daughter', 'sister', 'mother', 'niece', 'wife', 'bride', 'widow', 'heroine', 'hen', 'duck', 'vixen' and 'lioness' are feminine nouns. Similarly, 'table', 'chair', 'desk', 'carpet', 'window', 'lamp', 'car', 'shop', 'dress', 'tie', 'newspaper', 'book', 'building' and 'town' are all neuter.

Some nouns in English can refer either to a man or a woman, unless the sex is indicated in the context. Such neutral nouns are sometimes said to have DUAL GENDER. Examples include 'author', 'singer', 'poet', 'sculptor', 'proprietor', 'teacher', 'parent', 'cousin', 'adult' and 'child'. Some words in this category were formerly automatically assumed to be masculine and several of them had feminine forms, such as 'authoress', 'poetess', 'sculptress' and 'proprietrix'. In modern times this was felt to be sexist and many of these feminine forms are now rarely used, for example, 'authoress' and 'poetess'. However some, such as actress and waitress, are still in common use. See -ESS.

In many languages grammatical gender plays a major part. In French, for example, all nouns are divided into masculine and feminine, and there is no neuter classification. Masculine nouns are preceded by *le* (definite article). Thus 'ceiling' is masculine (*le plafond*), 'hat' is masculine (*le chapeau*) and 'book' is masculine (*le livre*). Feminine nouns are preceded by *la* (definite article). Thus 'door' is feminine (*la porte*), 'dress' is feminine (*la robe*), and 'window' is feminine (*la fenêtre*).

In German there are three grammatical genders—masculine, feminine and neuter. Masculine nouns are preceded by *der* (definite article) as *der Stuhl* (the chair); feminine nouns are preceded by *die* (definite article) as *die Brücke* (the bridge); neuter nouns are preceded by *das*, as *das Brot* (bread).

Grammatical gender in English is not relevant except in the third personal singular pronouns, as 'he/him/his/himself', 'she/her/hers/herself' and 'it/it/its/itself'. Traditionally 'he', etc, was considered an acceptable pronoun not just for nouns of the masculine gender, but also for those of neutral or dual gender as well. Thus 'Every student must check that he has registered for the exam' was considered acceptable, as was 'Each passenger must be responsible for his own luggage'. Nowadays such sentences are considered sexist. In order to avoid this, some people use the 'he/she', 'his/her', etc, convention, as in 'Every employee must supply his/her own transport' and 'Each candidate must hand in his/her application form now'. People who feel this is clumsy sometimes prefer to be ungrammatical and use a plural pronoun, as in 'Every writer was told to collect their manuscripts in person' and 'Every pupil was told that they would have to be back in school by four o'clock'. It is sometimes possible to avoid being both sexist and ungrammatical by rephrasing such sentences in the plural, as in 'All pupils were told that they would have to be back in school by four o'clock'.

genitive case

A case that indicates possession or ownership. It is usually marked by *s* and an apostrophe. Many spelling errors centre on the position of the *s* in relation to the apostrophe.

Nouns in the genitive case are usually formed by adding *'s* to the singular noun, as in 'the girl's mother', and Peter's car'; by adding an apostrophe to plural nouns that end in *s*, as in 'all the teachers' cars' and 'the doctors' surgeries'; by adding *'s* to irregular plural nouns that do not end in s, as in 'women's shoes'.

In the genitive form of a name or singular noun that ends in s, x or z, the apostrophe may or may not be followed by s. In words of one syllable the final s is usually added, as in 'James's house', 'the fox's lair', 'Roz's dress'.

The final s is most frequently omitted in names, particularly in names of three or more syllables, as in 'Euripides' plays'.

In many cases the presence or absence of final s is a matter of convention.

Apostrophes are often omitted wrongly in modern usage, particularly in the media and by advertisers, as in 'womens hairdressers', 'childrens helpings'. In addition, apostrophes are frequently added erroneously (as in 'potato's for sale' and 'Beware of the dog's'). This is partly because people are unsure about when and when not to use them and partly because of a modern tendency to punctuate as little as possible.

A group genitive occurs when more than one noun is involved, as in 'Gilbert and Sullivan's operas'. Note there is only one apostrophe s.

The alternative genitive construction involves the use of 'of', as in 'the mother of the girl', 'the uncle of the little girl', 'the pages of the newspaper' and 'the leg of the chair'. In general, proper nouns and animate beings tend to take the apostrophe and s ending and inanimate objects tend to take the 'of' construction.

geo-
A prefix derived from Greek indicating 'earth', as in geography, geology, geomagnetic and geophysics.

geographical features

These should be written with initial capital letters. They include the common nouns that are part of the name of the feature, as in Niagara Falls, Atlantic Ocean, River Thames, Mount Everest and Devil's Island.

gerund

The *-ing* form of a verb when it functions as a noun. It is sometimes known as a **verbal noun**. It has the same form as the present participle but has a different function. For example, in the sentence 'He was jogging down the road', 'jogging' is the present participle in the verb phrase 'was jogging', but in the sentence 'Running is his idea of relaxation', 'running' is a gerund because it acts as a noun as the subject of the sentence. Similarly, in the sentence 'We were smoking when the teacher found us', 'smoking' is the present participle in the verb phrase 'were smoking', but in the sentence 'We were told that smoking is bad for our health', 'smoking' is a gerund since it acts as a noun as the subject of the clause.

get

This verb is sometimes used to form the passive voice instead of the verb 'to be'. The use of the verb 'to get' to form the passive, as in 'They get married tomorrow', 'Our team got beaten today' and 'We got swindled by the con man' is sometimes considered to be more informal than the use of 'be'. Often there is more action involved when the get construction is used than when be is used, since get is a more dynamic verb, as in 'She was late leaving the pub because she got involved in an argument' and in 'It was her own fault that she got arrested by the police. She hit one of the constables'.

Get is frequently overused. Such overuse should be avoided, particularly in formal contexts. Get can often be replaced by a synonym such as 'obtain', 'acquire', 'receive', 'get hold of', etc. Thus, 'If you are getting into money difficulties you should get some financial advice. Perhaps you could get a bank loan' could be rephrased as 'If you are in financial difficulty you should obtain some financial help. Perhaps you could receive a bank loan'.

Got, the past tense of get, is often used unnecessarily, as in 'She has got red hair and freckles' and 'We have got enough food to last us the week'. In these sentences 'has' and 'have' are sufficient on their own.

gliding vowel means the same as **diphthong**.

goal
This can be used to describe the recipient of the action of a verb, the opposite of 'agent' or 'actor'. Thus, in the sentence 'The boy hit the girl', 'boy' is the 'agent' or 'actor' and 'girl' is the goal. Similarly, in the sentence 'The dog bit the postman', 'dog' is the 'agent' or 'actor' and 'postman' is the goal.

gobbledygook
A noun that is used informally to refer to pretentious and convoluted language of the type that is found in official documents and reports. It is extremely difficult to understand and should be avoided and 'plain English' used instead.

govern
A term that is used of a verb or preposition in relation to a

noun or pronoun to indicate that the verb or preposition has a noun or pronoun depending on it. Thus, in the phrase 'on the table', 'on' is said to govern 'table'.

gradable

A term that is used of adjectives and adverbs to mean that they can take degrees of comparison. Thus 'clean' is a gradable adjective since it has a comparative form (cleaner) and a superlative form (cleanest). 'Soon' is a gradable adverb since it has a comparative form (sooner) and a superlative form (soonest). Such words as 'supreme', which cannot normally have a comparative or superlative form, are called **non-gradable**.

-gram

A suffix derived from Greek indicating 'writing' or 'drawing', as in telegram, electrocardiogram and diagram. It is also used in modern usage to indicate a 'greeting' or 'message', as in kissogram.

-graph

A suffix derived from Greek indicating 'written, recorded, represented', as in autograph, monograph, photograph. It is also used to indicate 'an instrument that records', as in seismograph, tachograph and cardiograph.

group noun means the same as **collective noun**.

gynaec-, gynaeco-

A prefix derived from Greek indicating 'female, woman', as in gynaecology, gynaecium.

H

habitual

A term used to refer to the action of a verb that occurs regularly and repeatedly. The **habitual present** is found in such sentences as 'He goes to bed at ten every night', 'She always walks to work' and 'The old man sleeps all day'. This is in contrast to the **stative present**, which indicates the action of the verb that occurs at all times, as in 'Cows chew the cud', 'Water becomes ice when it freezes', 'Children grow up' and 'We all die'. Examples of the **habitual past** tense include; 'They travelled by train to work all their lives', 'We worked twelve hours a day on that project' and 'She studied night and day for the exams'.

-hand

A suffix meaning 'worker', as in deckhand, farmhand and cowhand. It can also mean 'position', as in right-hand and left-hand.

haem-, haemo-

A prefix derived from Greek meaning 'blood', as in haemorrhage, haematology and haematoma.

haiku

A short Japanese poem in three unrhymed lines with an exact

number of syllables per line, the syllable pattern being 5-7-5. The traditional subject matter is usually something to do with nature. A master of the form was the 17th-century Japanese poet Basho, and the following is one of his haiku:

The | white | chry|san|themum
Even | when | lif|ted | to | the | eye
Re|mains | im|macu|late.

half and halve

These are liable to be confused. **Half** is a noun and **halve** is a verb. Half is followed by a singular noun when it is referring to an amount, as in 'Half of the milk has gone sour' and 'Half the money is hers'. It is followed by a plural verb when it is referring to a number, as in 'Half of the people are still undecided' and 'Half of the sweets are for the younger children'. The plural of half is **halves**, as in 'They cut the oranges in two and distributed the halves to the members of the two teams'.

The plural noun halves is liable to be confused with the verb **halve**. Examples of the noun halves include 'They served halves of grapefruit for breakfast' and 'He split the estate into halves and left it to his son and daughter'. Examples of the verb halve include 'halve the grapefruit for breakfast' and 'He decided to halve his estate between his son and daughter'.

hanged and hung

These are both past tense and past participles of the verb 'to hang' but they are not interchangeable. **Hung** is the more usual form, as in 'The children hung their outdoor clothes on pegs outside the classroom', 'They hung the portrait of her father in the dining room', 'Dark clouds of smoke hung over the city' and 'The boy has hung around with the same crowd of friends for years'.

Hanged is restricted to the meaning 'suspended by the neck until dead', as in 'They hanged him for the murder of his wife in the 1920s', 'The murderer took his own life before he could be hanged', 'They had to break the news to the children that their father had hanged himself' and 'She hanged herself while the balance of her mind was disturbed'

hanging participle see **dangling participle**.

have
A verb that has several functions. A major use is its part in forming the 'perfect tense' and 'past perfect tense', or 'pluperfect tense', of other verb tenses. It does this in conjunction with the 'past participle' of the verb in question.

The perfect tense of a verb is formed by the present tense of the verb have and the past participle of the verb. Examples include 'We have acted wisely', 'They have beaten the opposition', 'The police have caught the thieves', 'The old man has died', 'The child has eaten all the food', 'The baby has fallen downstairs', 'They have grabbed all the bargains', 'You have hated him for years' and 'He has indicated that he is going to retire'. The past perfect or pluperfect is formed by the past tense of the verb have and the past participle of the verb in question, as in 'He had jumped over the fence', 'They had kicked in the door', 'The boy had led the other children to safety', 'His mother had made the cake', 'The headmaster had punished the pupils' and 'They had rushed into buying a new house'. Both perfect tenses and past perfect or pluperfect tenses are often contracted in speech or in informal written English, as in 'We've had enough for today', 'You've damaged the suitcase', 'You've missed the bus', 'He's lost his wallet', 'She's arrived too late', 'They'd left before the news came through', 'She'd married without telling her parents', 'He'd packed the goods himself' and 'You'd locked the door without realizing it'.

Have is often used in the phrase **have to** in the sense that something must be done. In the present tense have to can be used instead of 'must', as in 'You have to leave now', 'We have to clear this mess up', 'He has to get the next train' and 'The goods have to be sold today'. If the 'something that must be done' refers to the future the verb **will have to** is used', as in 'He will have to leave now to get there on time', 'The old man will have to go to hospital' and 'They'll have to move out of the house when her parents return'. If the 'something that must be done' refers to the past, **had to** is used, as in 'We had to take the injured man to hospital', 'They had to endure freezing conditions on the mountain', 'They'd to take a reduction in salary' and 'We'd to wait all day for the workman to appear'.

Have is also used in the sense of 'possess' or 'own', as in 'He has a swimming pool behind his house ', 'She has a huge wardrobe', 'We have enough food' and 'They have four cars'. In spoken or in informal English 'have got' is often used, as in 'They've got the largest house in the street', 'We've got problems now', 'They haven't got time'. This use should be avoided in formal English.

Have is also used to indicate suffering from an illness or disease, as in 'The child has measles', 'Her father has flu' and 'She has heart disease'. Have can also indicate that an activity is taking place, as in 'She's having a shower', 'We're having a party', 'She is having a baby' and 'They are having a dinner party'.

he

A personal pronoun that is used as the subject of a sentence or clause to refer to a man, boy, etc. It is thus said to be a 'masculine' personal pronoun. Since he refers to a third party and does not refer to the speaker or the person being addressed, it is a third-person pronoun. Examples include 'James is quite nice but he can be boring', 'Bob has got a new job and he is very pleased' and 'He is rich now but his parents are still very poor'.

He traditionally was used not only to refer to nouns relating to the masculine sex but also to nouns that are now regarded as being neutral or of DUAL GENDER. Such nouns include 'architect', 'artist', 'athlete', 'doctor', 'passenger', 'parent', 'pupil', 'singer', 'student'. Without further information from the context it is impossible to know to which sex such nouns are referring. In modern usage it is regarded as sexist to assume such words to be masculine by using he to refer to one of them unless the context indicates that the noun in question refers to a man or boy. Formerly it was considered acceptable to write or say 'Send a message to the architect who designed the building that he is to attend the meeting' whether or not the writer or speaker knew that the architect was a man. Similarly it was considered acceptable to write or say 'Please tell the doctor that he is to come straight away' whether or not the speaker or writer knew that the doctor was in fact a man. Nowadays this convention is considered sexist. In order to avoid sexism it is possible to use the convention 'he/she', as in

'Every pupil was told that he/she was to be smartly dressed for the occasion', 'Each passenger was informed that he/she was to arrive ten minutes before the coach was due to leave' and 'Tell the doctor that he/she is required urgently'. However this convention is regarded by some people as being clumsy, particularly in spoken English or in informal written English. Some people prefer to be ungrammatical and use the plural personal pronoun 'they' instead of 'he/she' in certain situations, as in 'Every passenger was told that they had to arrive ten minutes before the coach was due to leave' and 'Every student was advised that they should apply for a college place by March'. In some cases it may be possible to rephrase sentences and avoid being either sexist or ungrammatical, as in 'All the passengers were told that they should arrive ten minutes before the coach was due to leave' and 'All students were advised that they should apply for a college place by March'.

heading

A word, phrase or sentence put at the top of a page, chapter, section, etc, of a book or other printed document. These are sometimes written with initial capital letters (except for articles or prepositions), as in 'Annual Report', 'Department Budget for the Year', 'The Year Ahead', 'What Went Wrong', 'Company Plans', 'Trading Outlook Overseas', but this is a matter of taste or of house style of the company or organization involved. Some people prefer to use lower-case letters except for the first word, as in 'Sales targets for the year', 'A review of export markets', and 'The way forward'. Headings can be underlined or placed in italic type or bold type to highlight them on the page.

headline

The name given to the title of a newspaper article. From the very nature of headlines they are short, partly because of shortage of space and partly to capture the attention of the would-be reader. In order to achieve this, the definite and indefinite articles and other minor words tend to be omitted, the future tense represented by a to-infinitive, as in 'Prescription charges to rise', and the present tenses used for past events. **Headline language**, particularly that of tabloid newspapers which has to be especially succinct and eye-catching, can have an effect on the general language. Thus expressions such as 'tug-of-love', which describes the state of a child whose custody is being bitterly fought over by both parents, is now quite common in the general language but started out as a headline term. Other expressions that are typical of the language of the headlines include 'killing spree', which describes someone who loses control and kills, usually by shooting, several people indiscriminately, as in 'Local gunman goes on killing spree'. Another one is 'have-a-go', which describes an attempt by a member of the public to try and catch a criminal, as in 'Pensioner in have-a-go with bank-raider'. The language and style of headlines is frequently known as **headlinese**.

headword

A word that is at the head of an entry in a dictionary or other reference book. It is also known as 'entry word' and is usually written in bold type so that it stands out on the page and is readily identifiable.

helping verb another name for **auxiliary verb**.

hemi-
A prefix derived from Greek meaning 'half', as in hemisphere and hemiplegia.

hendiadys
A figure of speech in which two nouns joined by 'and' are used to express an idea that would normally be expressed by the use of an adjective and a noun, as in 'through storm and weather' instead of 'through stormy weather'.

he/she *see* **he**.

her
A personal pronoun. It is the third person singular, is feminine in gender and acts as the object in a sentence, as in 'We saw her yesterday', 'I don't know her', 'He hardly ever sees her', 'Please give this book to her', 'Our daughter sometimes plays with her' and 'We do not want her to come to the meeting'. *See* HE; SHE.

hers
A personal pronoun. It is the third person singular, feminine in gender and is in the poassessive case. 'The car is not hers', 'I have forgotten my book but I don't want to borrow hers', 'This is my seat and that is hers', and 'These clothes are hers'. *See* HIS; HER and POSSESSIVE.

hetero-
A prefix derived from Greek meaning 'other, another, different', as in heterodox and heterosexual.

hexa-
A prefix derived from Greek meaning 'six', as in hexagram and hexagon.

hiatus
A break in pronunciation between two vowels that come together in different syllables, as in 'Goyaesque' and 'cooperate'.

him
The third person masculine personal pronoun when used as the object of a sentence or clause, as in 'She shot him', 'When the police caught the thief they arrested him' and 'His parents punished him after the boy stole the money'. Traditionally him was used to apply not only to masculine nouns, such as 'man' and 'boy', but also to nouns that are said to be 'of dual gender'. These include 'architect', 'artist', 'parent', 'passenger', 'pupil' and 'student'. Without further information from the context, it is not possible for the speaker or writer to know the sex of the person referred to by one of these words. Formerly it was acceptable to write or say 'The artist must bring an easel with him' and 'Each pupil must bring food with him'. In modern usage this convention is considered sexist and there is a modern convention that 'him/her' should be used instead to avoid sexism, as in 'The artist must bring an easel with him/her' and 'Each pupil must bring food with 'him/her'. This convention is felt by some people to be clumsy, particularly in spoken and in informal English, and some people prefer to be ungrammatical and use the plural personal pronoun 'them' instead, as in 'The artist must bring an easel with them' and 'Each pupil must bring food with them'. In some situations it is possible to avoid

being either sexist or ungrammatical by rephrasing the sentence, as in 'All artists must bring easels with them' and 'All pupils must bring food with them. See HE.

him/her see **him**.

his

The third personal masculine pronoun when used to indicate possession, as in 'He has hurt his leg', 'The boy has taken his books home' and 'Where has your father left his tools?' Traditionally his was used to refer not only to masculine nouns, such as 'man', 'boy', etc, but to what are known as nouns 'of dual gender'. These include 'architect', 'artist', 'parent', 'passenger', 'pupil' and 'student'. Without further information from the context it is not possible for the speaker or the writer to know the sex of the person referred to by one of these words. Formerly it was considered acceptable to use his in such situations, as in 'Every pupil has to supply his own sports equipment' and 'Every passenger is responsible for his own luggage'. In modern usage this is now considered sexist and there is a modern convention that 'his/her' should be used instead to avoid sexism, as in 'Every pupil has to supply his/her own sports equipment' and 'Every passenger is responsible for his/her own luggage'. This convention is felt by some people to be clumsy, particularly when used in spoken or informal written English. Some people prefer to be ungrammatical and use the plural personal pronoun 'their', as in 'Every pupil must supply their own sports equipment' and 'Every passenger is to be responsible for their own luggage'. In some situations it is possible to avoid being sexist, clumsy and ungrammatical by rephrasing the sentence, as in 'All pupils must supply their own sports equipment' and 'All passengers are to be responsible for their own luggage.

his/her *see* **his.**

holidays
These, in the sense of public holidays or festivals, should be written with an initial capital letter, as in Christmas Day, Easter Sunday, New Year and Independence Day.

holo-
A prefix meaning 'complete, whole', as in holistic.

homo-
A prefix derived from Greek meaning 'same', as in homogenous, homonym, homograph, homology, homophone and homosexual.

homograph
A word that is spelt the same as another word but has a different meaning and pronunciation. Homographs include:

bow, pronounced to rhyme with 'how', a verb meaning 'to bend the head or body as a sign of respect or in greeting, etc', as in 'The visitors bowed to the emperor' and 'The mourners bowed their heads as the coffin was lowered into the grave'.

bow, pronounced to rhyme with 'low', a noun meaning 'a looped knot, a ribbon tied in this way', as in 'She tied her hair in a bow' and 'She wears blue bows in her hair'.

lead, pronounced 'leed', a verb meaning 'to show the way', as in 'The guide will lead you down the mountain'.

lead, pronounced 'led', a noun meaning 'a type of greyish metal', as in 'They are going to remove any water pipes made from lead'.

row, pronounced to rhyme with 'low', a noun meaning 'a number of people or things arranged in a line', as in 'The princess sat in the front row'.

row, pronounced to rhyme with 'how', a noun meaning 'a quarrel, a disagreement', as in 'He has had a row with his neighbour over repairs to the garden wall'.

slough, pronounced to rhyme with 'rough', a verb meaning 'to cast off', as in 'The snake had sloughed off its old skin'.

slough, pronounced to rhyme with 'how', a noun meaning 'a swamp', as in 'Get bogged down in a slough' and 'in the Slough of Despond'.

sow, pronounced to rhyme with 'low', a verb meaning 'to scatter seeds in the earth', as in 'In the spring the gardener sowed some flower seeds in the front garden'.

sow, pronounced to rhyme with 'how', a noun meaning 'a female pig', as in 'The sow is in the pigsty with her piglets'.

homonym

A word that has the same spelling and the same pronunciation as another word but has a different meaning from it. Examples include:

bill, a noun meaning 'a written statement of money owed', as in 'You must pay the bill for the conversion work immediately', or 'a written or printed advertisement', as in 'We were asked to deliver handbills advertising the play'.

bill, a noun meaning 'a bird's beak', as in 'The seagull has injured its bill'.

fair, an adjective meaning 'attractive', as in 'fair young women'; 'light in colour', as in 'She has fair hair'; 'fine, not raining', as in 'I hope it keeps fair'; 'just, free from prejudice', as in 'We felt that the referee came to a fair decision'.

fair, a noun meaning 'a market held regularly in the same place, often with stalls, entertainments and rides' (now often simply applying to an event with entertainments and rides without the market), as in 'He won a coconut at the fair'; 'a trade exhibition', as in 'the Frankfurt Book Fair'.

pulse, a noun meaning 'the throbbing caused by the contractions of the heart', as in 'The patient has a weak pulse'.

pulse, a noun meaning 'the edible seeds of any of various crops of the pea family, as lentils, peas and beans', as in 'Vegetarians eat a lot of food made with pulses'.

row, a verb meaning 'to propel a boat by means of oars', as in 'He plans to row across the Atlantic single-handed'.

row, a noun meaning 'a number of people or things arranged in a line', as in 'We tried to get into the front row to watch the procession' and 'The gardener has planted rows of cabbages'.

homophone

The term for a word that is pronounced in the same way as another but is spelt in a different way and has a different meaning. Some examples of homophones include the following:

aisle, a noun meaning 'a passage between rows of seats in a church, theatre, cinema etc', as in 'The bride walked down the aisle on her father's arm'.

isle, a noun meaning 'an island', as in 'the Isle of Wight'.

alter, a verb meaning 'to change', as in 'They have had to alter their plans'.

altar, a noun meaning 'in the Christian church, the table on which the bread and wine are consecrated for Communion and which serves as the centre of worship', as in 'The priest moved to the altar, from where he dispensed Communion', 'There is a holy painting above the altar'; or 'a raised structure on which sacrifices are made or incense burned in worship', as in 'The Druids made human sacrifices on the altar of their gods'.

ail, a verb meaning 'to be ill', as in 'The old woman is ailing'; 'to be the matter, to be wrong', as in 'What ails you?'

ale, a noun meaning 'a kind of beer', as in 'a pint of foaming ale'.

blew, a verb, the past tense of the verb 'blow', as in 'They blew the trumpets loudly'.

blue, a noun and adjective meaning 'a colour of the shade of a clear sky', as in 'She wore a blue dress'.

boar, a noun meaning 'a male pig', as in 'a dish made with wild boar'.

bore, a verb meaning 'to make tired and uninterested', as in 'The audience was obviously bored by the rather academic lecture'.

bore, a verb, the past tense of the verb 'bear', as in 'They bore their troubles lightly'.

cereal, a noun meaning 'a plant yielding grain suitable for food', as in 'countries which grow cereal crops' and 'a prepared food made with grain', as in 'We often have cereal for breakfast'.

serial, a noun meaning 'a story or television play which is published or appears in regular parts, as in 'the final instalment of the magazine serial which she was following'.

cite, a verb meaning 'to quote or mention by way of example or proof', as in 'The lawyer cited a previous case to try and get his client off'.

sight, a noun meaning 'the act of seeing', as in 'They recognized him at first sight'.

site, a noun meaning 'a location, place', as in 'They have found a site for the new factory'.

feat, a noun meaning 'a notable act or deed', as in 'The old man received an award for his courageous feat'.

feet, a noun, the plural form of 'foot', as in 'The child got her feet wet from wading in the puddle'.

none, a pronoun meaning 'not any', as in 'They are demanding money but we have none'.

nun, a noun meaning 'a woman who joins a religious order and takes vows of poverty, chastity and obedience', as in 'She gave up the world to become a nun'.

know, a verb meaning 'to have understanding or knowledge of', as in 'He is the only one who knows the true facts of the situation', and 'to be acquainted with', as in 'I met her once but I don't really know her'.

no, an adjective meaning 'not any', as in 'We have no food left'.

rite, a noun meaning 'a ceremonial act or words,' as in 'rites involving witchcraft'.

right, an adjective meaning 'correct', as in 'Very few people gave the right answer to the question'.

write, a verb meaning 'to form readable characters', as in 'he writes regularly for the newspapers'.

stare, a verb and noun meaning 'to look fixedly' and 'a fixed gaze', as in 'She stared at him in disbelief when he told her the news' and 'He has the stare of a basilisk'.

stair, a noun meaning 'a series of flights of stairs', as in 'The old lady is too feeble to climb the stairs to her bedroom'.

-hood

A suffix meaning 'state, condition', as in babyhood, childhood, manhood, priesthood, womanhood and widowhood.

hybrid

A word that is formed from words or elements derived from different languages, such as 'television'.

hydro-

A prefix derived from Greek meaning 'water, as in hydro-electric and hydrophobia. It also means 'hydrogen', as in hydrochloride.

hyper-

A prefix derived from Greek meaning 'over, above', as in hyperbole, hyperactive, hypercritical, hyperinflation and hypersensitive.

hyperbole

A figure of speech consisting of exaggeration or over-statement, used for emphasis, as in 'I could eat a horse' and in 'I am boiling in this heat'.

hyphen

A small stroke (-) that is used to join two words together or to indicate that a word has been broken at the end of a line because of lack of space. It is used in a variety of situations.

The hyphen is used as the prefixed element in a proper noun, as in 'pre-Christian', 'post-Renaissance', 'anti-British', 'anti-Semitic', 'pro-French' and 'pro-Marxism'. It is also used before dates or numbers, as in 'pre-1914', 'pre-1066', 'post-1920', 'post-1745'. It is also used before abbreviations, as in 'pro-BBC', 'anti-EEC' and 'anti-TUC'.

The hyphen is used for clarification. Some words are ambiguous without the presence of a hyphen. For example, 're-cover', as in 're-cover a chair', is spelt with a hyphen to differentiate it from 'recover', as in 'The accident victim is likely to recover'. Similarly, it is used in 're-form', meaning 'to form again', as in 'They have decided to re-form the society which closed last year', to differentiate the word from 'reform', meaning 'to improve, to become better behaved', as in 'He was wild as a young man but he has reformed now'. Similarly 're-count' in the sense of 'count again', as in 're-count the number of votes cast', is spelt with a hyphen to differentiate it from 'recount' in the sense of 'tell', as in 'recount what happened on the night of the accident'.

The hyphen was formerly used to separate a prefix from the main element of a word if the main element begins with a vowel, as in 'pre-eminent', but there is a growing tendency in modern usage to omit the hyphen in such cases. At the moment both 'pre-eminent' and 'preeminent' are found. However, if the omission of the hyphen results in double *i*, the hyphen is usually retained, as in 'anti-inflationary' and 'semi-insulated'.

The hyphen was formerly used in words formed with the prefix *non-*, as in 'non-functional', 'non-political', 'non-flammable' and 'non-pollutant'. However there is a growing tendency to omit the hyphen in such cases, as in 'nonfunctional' and 'nonpollutant'. At the moment both forms of such words are common.

The hyphen is usually used with 'ex-' in the sense of 'former', as in 'ex-wife' and 'ex-president'.

The hyphen is usually used when 'self-' is prefixed to words, as in 'self-styled', 'a self-starter' and 'self-evident'.

Use or non-use of the hyphen is often a matter of choice, house style or frequency of usage, as in 'drawing-room' or 'drawing room', and 'dining-room' or 'dining room'. There is a modern tendency to punctuate less frequently than was formerly the case and so in modern usage use of the hyphen in such expressions is less frequent. The length of compounds often affects the inclusion or omission of the hyphen. Compounds of two short elements that are well-established words tend not to be hyphenated, as in 'bedroom' and 'toothbrush'. Compound words with longer elements are more likely to be hyphenated, as in 'engine-driver' and 'carpet-layer'.

Some fixed compounds of two or three or more words are always hyphenated, as in 'son-in-law', 'good-for-nothing' and 'devil-may-care'

Some compounds formed from phrasal verbs are sometimes hyphenated and sometimes not. Thus both 'take-over' and 'takeover' are common, and 'run-down' and 'rundown' are both common. Again the use of the hyphen is a matter of choice. However some words formed from phrasal verbs are usually spelt without a hyphen, as in 'breakthrough'.

Compound adjectives consisting of two elements, the second of which ends in -ed, are usually hyphenated, as in 'heavy-hearted', 'fair-haired', 'fair-minded' and 'long-legged'.

Compound adjectives when they are used before nouns are

usually hyphenated, as in 'gas-fired central heating', 'oil-based paints', 'solar-heated buildings' and 'chocolate-coated biscuits'.

Compounds containing some adverbs are usually hyphenated, sometimes to avoid ambiguity, as in 'his best-known opera', a 'well-known singer', 'an ill-considered venture' and 'a half-planned scheme'.

Generally adjectives and participles preceded by an adverb are not hyphenated if the adverb ends in -ly, as in 'a highly talented singer', 'neatly pressed clothes' and 'beautifully dressed young women'.

In the case of two or more compound hyphenated adjectives with the same second element qualifying the same noun, the common element need not be repeated but the hyphen should be, as in 'two- and three-bedroom houses' and 'long- and short-haired dogs'.

The hyphen is used in compound numerals from 21 to 99 when they are written in full, as in 'thirty-five gallons', 'forty-four years', 'sixty-seven miles' and 'two hundred and forty-five miles'. Compound numbers such as 'three hundred' and 'two thousand' are not hyphenated.

Hyphens are used in fractions, as in 'three-quarters', 'two-thirds', and 'seven-eighths'.

Hyphens are also used in such number phrases as 'a seventeenth-century play', 'a sixteenth-century church', 'a five-gallon pail', 'a five-year contract' and a 'third-year student'.

The other use of hyphens is to break words at the ends of lines. Formerly people were more careful about where they broke words. Previously, words were broken up according to etymological principles, but there is a growing tendency to break words according to how they are pronounced. Some dictionaries or spelling dictionaries give help with the division and hyphenation of individual words. General points are that one-syllable words should not be divided and words should not be broken after the first letter of a word or before the last letter. Care should be taken not to break up words, for example by forming elements that are words in their own right, in such a way as to mislead the reader. Thus divisions such as 'the-rapist' and 'mans-laughter' should be avoided.

hypo-

A prefix derived from Greek meaning 'under', as in hypothermia, hypodermic.

I

I and me

These are liable to be confused. They are both parts of the first person singular pronoun, but I acts as the subject of a sentence and me as the object. People often assume wrongly that me is less 'polite' than I. This is probably because they have been taught that in answer to such questions as 'Who is there?' the grammatically correct reply is 'It is I'. In fact, except in formal contexts, 'It is me' is frequently found in modern usage, especially in spoken contexts. Confusion arises as to whether to use I or me after 'between'. Since 'between' is followed by an object, me is the correct form. Thus it is correct to say 'Just between you and me, I think he is dishonest'. On the other hand, me, being an object, should not be used in such sentences as 'You and I have both been invited', 'May Jane and I play?' and 'The children and I are going to join you'. Me should, however, be used in such sentences as 'The cake was made by Mary and me', 'They were sitting in front of my son and me at the cinema' and 'My brother and father played against my mother and me', since in all these cases it is the object form of the first person singular that is required.

-ian

A suffix either indicating 'a profession, job or pastime', as in comedian, musician, optician, physician, or indicating 'proper names', as in Dickensian, Orwellian and Shakesperian.

-iana

A suffix form of -ANA, indicating 'memorabilia or collections relating to people or places of note', as in Victoriana and Churchilliana.

-ible *see* **adjectives**.

-ics

A suffix indicating 'science' or 'study', as in 'acoustics', 'electronics', 'genetics', 'obstetrics', 'politics' and 'physics'.

ideogram

A written character that symbolizes a word or phrase without indicating the pronunciation, such as £, &, +.

idiolect

The speech habits, knowledge and command of language of an individual. This can vary considerably from person to person. For example, one person might have a much more formal idiolect than another.

idiom

An expression whose meaning cannot be easily deduced from the individual meanings of the words it contains. Thus, in the expression 'know the ropes' one can know what 'know' means and know what 'ropes' means without being able to deduce the meaning of 'know the ropes'. In fact, 'know the ropes' is a nautical idiom. If a sailor was being taught the basics of sea-manship in the days of sailing ships, he would have to be taught the mechanics of ropes which were an important part of sail-ing in those days. Hence, 'know the ropes' has come to mean 'to understand the procedures and details involved in some-thing', as in 'When he first started the job the trainee me-chanic felt really awkward and useless, but he when he knew the ropes he felt more confident and happier'.

Similarly, one can easily understand the meanings of the vari-ous individual words in the expression 'out on a limb', but it is not at all obvious that it means idiomatically 'in a risky and of-ten lonely position', this being a reference to someone being stuck in an isolated and precarious position on the branch of a tree. This idiom is found in sentences such as 'The young de-signer has gone out on a limb and produced clothes that his boss says are too experimental for the mass market'. Literally it refers to a person or animal that has crawled so far out on a branch of a tree that he/she is in danger of falling or of not being able to crawl back to the main tree.

Similarly, in the expression 'throw someone to the lions' one can easily understand the meanings of the various individual words without realizing that the expression means 'deliber-ately to put someone in a difficult or dangerous position', as in 'All the teachers were responsible for the change in policy with regard to school uniform but they threw the deputy head to the lions when they asked him to address a parents' meet-ing on the subject'. In order to appreciate the meaning of the idiom fully, the reader or listener has to understand that the idiom refers to a supposed form of entertainment in ancient Rome in which prisoners were thrown to hungry wild animals to be attacked and killed (while spectators looked on enthusiastically).

Similarly, in the expression 'throw in the towel' one can easily understand the meanings of the various individual words without realizing that the phrase means 'to give in, to admit defeat', as in 'She tried to stand up to the bullies in her school but finally she threw in the towel and asked her parents to send her to another school'. This idiom comes from the world of boxing in which 'throwing in the towel' indicates a method of conceding defeat.

Similarly, understanding the individual words of the expression 'sell someone down the river' will not help one to understand that it means 'to betray or be disloyal to someone', as in 'The bank robber who was caught by the police refused to sell his associates down the river'. The origin here is slightly more obscure in that it refers historically to slave owners in the Mississippi states of the United States, who sold their slaves to buyers downstream in Louisiana where living and working conditions were much harder.

Such idioms as 'sell someone down the river' are known as 'opaque idioms' since there is no resemblance between the meaning of the individual words of the idiom and the idiom itself. Idioms such as 'keep a straight face' are known as 'transparent idioms' since, although they are not to be interpreted literally, it is reasonably obvious what they mean.

i.e.

The abbreviation of the Latin phrase *id est*, which is used before explanations or amplifications of what has just been mentioned, as in 'He was a mercenary in the war, i.e. he fought for money' and 'She is agoraphobic, i.e. she is afraid of open spaces' and 'He is a bibliophile, i.e. he loves books'. It is usually spelt with a full stop after each of the letters.

if

A CONJUNCTION that is often used to introduce a subordinate ADVERBIAL CLAUSE of condition, as in 'If he is talking of leaving he must be unhappy', 'If you tease the dog it will bite you', 'If he had realized that the weather was going to be so bad he would not have gone on the expedition', 'If I had been in charge I would have sacked him' and 'If it were a better organized firm things like that would not happen'.

If can also introduce a 'nominal' or 'noun clause', as in 'He asked if we objected' and 'She inquired if we wanted to go'.

-ify

A suffix indicating 'making or becoming', as in beautify, clarify, dignify, purify, satisfy and simplify.

imperative mood

The verb mood that expresses commands. The verbs in the following sentences are in the imperative mood: 'Go away!', 'Run faster!', 'Answer me!', 'Sit down!', 'Please get out of here!'. All of these expressions with verbs in the imperative mood sound rather imperious or dictatorial and usually end with an exclamation mark, but this is not true of all expressions with verbs in the imperative mood. For example, the following sentences all have verbs in the imperative mood: 'Have another helping of ice cream', 'Help yourself to more wine', 'Just follow the yellow arrows to the X-ray department', and

'Turn right at the roundabout'. Sentences with verbs in the imperative mood are known as **imperative sentences**.

imperfect

A TENSE that denotes an action in progress but not complete. The term derives from the classification in Latin grammar and was traditionally applied to the 'past imperfect', as in 'They were standing there'. The imperfect has now been largely superseded by the progressive/continuous tense, which is marked by the use of 'be' plus the present participle. Continuous tenses are used when talking about temporary situations at a particular point in time, as in 'They were waiting for the bus'.

impersonal

A verb that is used with a formal subject, usually 'it', as in 'It is raining' and 'They say it will snow tomorrow'.

indefinite article

A and **an** are the forms of the indefinite article. The form a is used before words that begin with a consonant sound, as 'a box', 'a garden', 'a road', 'a wall'. The form an is used before words that begin with a vowel sound, as 'an apple', 'an easel', 'an ostrich', 'an uncle'. Note that it is the sound of the initial letter that matters and not the spelling. Thus a is used before words beginning with a *u* when they are pronounced with a *y* sound as though it were a consonant, as 'a unit', 'a usual occurrence'. Similarly, an is used, for example, before words beginning with the letter *h* where this is not pronounced, as in 'an heir', 'an hour', 'an honest man'.

Formerly it was quite common to use an before words that begin with an *h* sound and also begin with an unstressed syllable, as in 'an hotel (*ho-tel*)', 'an historic (*his-tor-ik*) occasion', 'an hereditary (*her-ed-it-ary*) disease'. It is now more usual to use a in such cases and ignore the question of the unstressed syllable.

indefinite pronouns

These are used refer to people or things without being specific as to exactly who or what they are. They include 'everyone', 'everybody', 'everything', 'anyone', 'anybody', 'anything', 'somebody', 'someone', 'something' and 'nobody', 'no one', 'nothing', as in 'Everyone is to make a contribution', 'Anyone can enter', 'Something will turn up' and 'Nobody cares'.

independent clause

A clause that can stand alone and make sense without being dependent on another clause, as in 'The children are safe'. MAIN CLAUSEs are independent clauses. Thus in the sentence 'She is tired and she wants to go home', there are two independent clauses joined by 'and'. In the sentence 'She will be able to rest when she gets home', 'She will be able to rest' is an independent clause and 'when she gets home' is a DEPENDENT CLAUSE. In the sentence 'Because she is intelligent she thinks for herself', 'she thinks for herself' is an independent clause and 'because she is intelligent' is a dependent clause.

indicative mood

The MOOD of a verb which denotes making a statement. The following sentences have verbs in the indicative mood: 'We go on holiday tomorrow', 'He was waiting for her husband', 'They have lost the match' and 'She will arrive this afternoon'. The indicative mood is sometimes known as the **declarative mood**. The other moods are THE IMPERATIVE MOOD and SUBJUNCTIVE MOOD.

indirect object

An object that can be preceded by 'to' or 'for'. The indirect object usually refers to the person who benefits from an action or receives something as the result of it. In the sentence 'Her father gave the boy food', 'boy' is the indirect object and 'food' is the DIRECT OBJECT. The sentence could be rephrased as 'Her father gave food to the boy'. In the sentence 'He bought his mother flowers', 'his mother' is the indirect object and 'flowers' is the direct object. The sentence could have been rephrased as 'He bought flowers for his mother'. In the sentence 'They offered him a reward', 'him' is the indirect object and 'reward' is the direct object. The sentence could be rephrased as 'They offered a reward to him'.

indirect question

A question that is reported in INDIRECT SPEECH, as in 'We asked them where they were going', 'They inquired why we had come' and 'They looked at us curiously and asked where we had come from'. Note that a question mark is not used.

indirect speech also known as **reported speech**

A way of reporting what someone has said without using the actual words used by the speaker. There is usually an introductory verb and a subordinate 'that' clause, as in 'He said that he was going away', 'They announced that they were leaving next day' and 'She declared that she had seen him there before'. In DIRECT SPEECH these sentences would become 'He said, "I am going away"', 'They announced, "We are leaving tomorrow"' and 'She declared, "I have seen him there before"'. When the change is made from direct speech to indirect speech, the pronouns, adverbs of time and place and tenses are changed to accord with the viewpoint of the person doing the reporting.

infinitive

The BASE form of a verb when used without any indication of person, number or tense. There are two forms of the infinitive. One is the **to infinitive** form, as in 'They wished to leave', 'I plan to go tomorrow', 'We aim to please' and 'They want to emigrate', 'To know all is to forgive all', 'To err is human', 'Pull the lever to open', 'You should bring a book to read', 'The child has nothing to do', 'She is not very nice to know' and 'It is hard to believe that it happened'. The other form of the infinitive is called the **bare infinitive**. This form consists of the base form of the verb without 'to', as in 'We saw him fall', 'She watched him go', 'They noticed him enter', 'She heard him sigh', 'They let him go', 'I had better leave' and 'Need we return' and 'we dare not go back'. See SPLIT INFINITIVE.

inflect

When applied to a word, this means to change form in order to indicate differences of tense, number, gender, case, etc. Nouns inflect for plural, as in 'ships', 'chairs', 'houses' and 'oxen'; nouns inflect for possessive, as in 'boys'', 'woman's', 'teachers'', and 'parents''; some adjectives inflect for the comparative form, as in 'brighter', 'clearer', 'shorter' and 'taller'; verbs inflect for the third person singular present tense, as in 'hears', 'joins', 'touches' and 'kicks'; verbs inflect for the present participle, as in 'hearing', 'joining', 'touching' and 'kicking'; verbs inflect for the past participle, as in 'heard', 'joined', 'touched' and 'kicked'.

inflection

The act of inflecting—see INFLECT. It also refers to an inflected form of a word or a suffix or other element used to inflect a word.

informal

The term to describe a spoken or written style of language that has a simpler grammatical structure and simpler vocabulary, often involving vocabulary that is colloquial in nature or even slang.

infra-

A prefix derived from Latin indicating 'below, beneath', as in infrared and infrastructure.

-ing form

This form of a verb can be either a PRESENT PARTICIPLE or A gerund. Present participles are used in the formation of the progressive or continuous TENSES, as in 'We were looking at the pictures', 'Children were playing in the snow', 'They are waiting for the bus', 'Parents were showing their anger', 'He has been sitting there for hours'. Present participles can also be used in non-finite clauses or phrases, as in 'Walking along, she did not have a care in the world', 'Lying there, he thought about his life', 'Sighing, he left the room' and 'Smiling broadly he congratulated his friend'.

A large number of adjectives end in -ing. Many of these have the same form as the present participle of a transitive verb and are similar in meaning. Examples include 'an amazing spectacle', 'a boring show', 'an interesting idea', 'a tiring day', 'an exhausting climb' and 'aching limbs'. Some -ing adjectives are related to intransitive verbs, as 'existing problems', 'increasing responsibilities', 'dwindling resources', 'an ageing work force' and 'prevailing circumstances'. Some -ing adjectives are related to the forms of verbs but have different meanings from the verbs, as in 'becoming dress', 'an engaging personality', 'a dashing young man' and 'a retiring disposition'. Some -ing adjectives are not related to verbs at all. These include 'appetizing', 'enterprising', 'impending' and 'balding'. Some -ing adjectives are used informally for emphasis, as in 'a blithering idiot', 'a stinking cold' and 'a flaming cheek'.

Gerunds act as nouns and are sometimes known as **verbal nouns**. Examples include 'Smoking is bad for one's health', 'Cycling is forbidden in the park' and 'Swimming is his favourite sport'.

intensifier

The term for an adverb that affects the degree of intensity of another word. Intensifiers include 'thoroughly' in 'We were thoroughly shocked by the news', 'scarcely' in 'We scarcely recognized them' and 'totally' in 'She was totally amazed'.

inter-

A prefix of Latin origin indicating 'between', as in intercity, intercontinental and interstate.

interjection

A kind of EXCLAMATION. Sometimes they are formed by actual words and sometimes they simply consist of sounds indicating emotional noises. Examples of interjections include 'Oh! I am quite shocked', 'Gosh! I'm surprised to hear that!', 'Phew! It's hot!', 'Ouch! That was my foot!', 'Tut-tut! He shouldn't have done that!' and 'Alas! She is dead.'

International Phonetic Alphabet

A system of written symbols designed to enable the speech sounds of any language to be consistently represented. Some of the symbols are the ordinary letters of the Roman alphabet but some have been specially invented. The alphabet was first published in 1889 and is commonly known a **IPA**.

interrogative adjective or determiner

An adjective or determiner that asks for information in relation to the nouns which it qualifies, as in 'What dress did you choose in the end?', 'What kind of book are you looking for?', 'Which house do you like best?', 'Which pupil won the prize?', 'Whose bike was stolen?' and 'Whose dog is that?'

interrogative adverb

An adverb that asks a question, as in 'When did they leave?', 'When does the meeting start?', 'Where do they live?', 'Where was the stolen car found?', 'Where did you last see her?', 'Why was she crying?', 'Why have they been asked to leave?', 'How is the invalid?', 'How do you know that she has gone?' and 'Wherever did you find that?'

interrogative pronoun

A pronoun that asks a question, as in 'Who asked you to do

that?', 'Who broke the vase?', 'What did he say?, 'What happened next?', 'Whose are those books?', 'Whose is that old car?', 'To whom was that remark addressed?' and 'To whom did you address the package?'

interrogative sentence

A sentence that asks a question, as in 'Who is that?', 'Where is he?', 'Why have they appeared?', 'What did they take away?, 'Which do you prefer?' and 'Whose baby is that?'. Sentences that take the form of an interrogative question do not always seek information. Sometimes they are exclamations, as in 'Did you ever see anything so beautiful?', 'Isn't she sweet?' and 'Aren't they lovely?'. Sentences that take the form of questions may really be commands or directives, as in 'Could you turn down that radio?', 'Would you make less noise?' and 'Could you get her a chair?'. Sentences that take the form of questions may function as statements, as in 'Isn't there always a reason?' and 'Haven't we all experienced disappointment?'. Some interrogative sentences are what are known as RHETORICAL QUESTIONS, which are asked purely for effect and require no answer, as in 'Do you think I am a fool?', 'What is the point of life?' and 'What is the world coming to?'.

intra-

A prefix of Latin origin indicating 'within', as intramuscular, intra-uterine and intravenous.

intransitive verb

A verb that does not take a DIRECT OBJECT, as in 'Snow fell yesterday', 'The children played in the sand', 'The path climbed steeply', 'Time will tell', 'The situation worsened', 'Things im-

proved' and 'Prices increased'. Many verbs can be either TRANSI-
TIVE or intransitive, according to the context. Thus 'play' is intransitive in the sentence 'The children played in the sand' but
transitive in the sentence 'The boy plays the piano'. Similarly
'climb' is intransitive in the sentence 'The path climbs steeply'
but transitive in the sentence 'The mountaineers climbed Everest'. Similarly 'tell' is intransitive in the sentence 'Time will tell'
but transitive in the sentence 'He will tell his life story'.

introductory it

The use of 'it' as the subject of a sentence in the absence of a
meaningful subject. It is used particularly in sentences about
time and the weather, as in 'It is midnight', 'It is dawn', 'It is five
o'clock', 'It is twelve noon', 'It is raining', 'It was snowing', 'It
was windy' and 'It was blowing a gale'.

intrusive r

The pronunciation of the *r* sound between two words or syllables where the first of these ends in a vowel sound and the
second begins with a vowel sound and where there is no 'r' in
the spelling. It appears in such phrases as 'law and order',
which is frequently pronounced as 'lawr and order'.

invariable

A word whose form does not vary by inflection. Such words
include 'sheep' and 'but'.

inversion

The reversal of the usual word order. It particularly refers to
subjects and verbs. Inversion is used in questions, in some

negative sentences, and for literary effect. In questions, an
AUXILIARY VERB is usually put in front of the subject and the rest
of the verb group is put after the subject, as in 'Are you going
to see her?' and 'Have they inspected the goods yet?'. The verb
'to do' is frequently used in inversion, as in 'Did he commit the
crime?' and 'Do they still believe that?'. Examples of the use of
inversion in negative sentences include 'Seldom have I wit-
nessed such an act of selfishness', 'Never had she experienced
such pain' and 'Rarely do we have time to admire the beauty of
the countryside'. This use in negative sentences is rather formal.

Inversion frequently involves adverbial phrases of place, as in
'Beyond the town stretched field after field', 'Above them
soared the eagle' and 'Along the driveway grew multitudes of
daffodils'.

Inversion is also found in conditional clauses that are not introduced by conjunction, as in 'Had you arrived earlier you
would have got a meal' and 'Had we some more money we
could do more for the refugees'.

inverted commas, or **quotation marks** or **quotes**
These are used to enclose material that is part of DIRECT
SPEECH. They can also be used instead of italic type in the titles
of books, newspapers, magazines, plays, films, musical works,
works of art, etc, as in 'The Times', 'Northanger Abbey' by Jane
Austen, 'Two Gentlemen of Verona', 'The Silence of the Lambs'
and 'The Mikado'. Inverted commas can also be used to emphasize or draw attention to a particular word or phrase, as in
'She wants to know how to spell "picnicked"'. Inverted commas can either be single or double. If a word, phrase or pas-

sage is already contained within quotes, one should use the opposite style of inverted commas to the set already in use, as in 'She asked how to pronounce "controversy"' or "She asked how to pronounce 'controversy'".

IPA *see* **International Phonetic Alphabet.**

irony

The use of a word or words to convey something that is completely different from the literal meaning, as in 'I don't suppose you'd be interested to hear that your house has been burgled', 'So you've crashed the car. Thanks! That's a great help!' *See also* DRAMATIC IRONY.

irregular adjective

An adjective that does not conform to the usual rules of forming the comparative and superlative (see COMPARISON OF ADJECTIVES). Many adjectives either add -er for the comparative and -est for the superlative, as in 'taller', 'shorter' and 'tallest', 'shortest' from 'tall' and 'short'. Some adjectives form their comparatives with 'more' and their superlatives with 'most', as in 'more beautiful', 'more practical' and 'most beautiful', 'most practical'. Irregular adjectives do not form their comparatives and superlatives in either of these ways. Irregular adjectives include:

positive	*comparative*	*superlative*
good	better	best
bad	worse	worst
little	less	least
many	more	most

irregular plural

The plural form of a noun that does not form its plural in the regular way. Most nouns in English add -s to the singular form to form the plural form, as in 'boy' to 'boys'. Some add -es to the singular form to form the plural, as in 'church' to 'churches'. Nouns ending in a consonant followed by -y have -ies as a regular plural ending. Thus 'fairy' becomes 'fairies' and 'berry' becomes 'berries'. The foregoing are all examples of regular plurals.

Irregular plurals include words that are different in form from the singular forms and do not simply add an ending. These include 'men' from 'man', 'women' from 'woman' and 'mice' from 'mouse'. Some irregular plurals are formed by changing the vowel of the singular forms, as in 'feet' from 'foot', 'geese' from 'goose' and 'teeth' from 'tooth'. Some irregular plural forms are formed by adding -en, as 'oxen' from 'ox' and 'children' from 'child'. Some nouns ending in -f form plurals in -ves, as in 'loaf' to 'loaves', 'half' to 'halves', 'wife' to 'wives' and 'wolf' to 'wolves', but some have alternative endings, as 'hoof' to either 'hoofs' or 'hooves', and some form regular plurals unchanged, as 'roof' to 'roofs'. Some irregular plural forms are the original foreign plural forms of words adopted into English, for example 'stimuli' from 'stimulus', 'phenomena' from 'phenomenon', 'criteria' from 'criterion', 'larvae' from 'larva'. In modern usage there is a growing tendency to anglicize the plural forms of foreign words. Many of these co-exist with the plural form, for example 'thesauruses' and 'thesauri', 'formulas' and 'formulae', 'gateaus' and 'gateaux' and 'indexes' and 'indices'. Sometimes the anglicized plural formed according to the regular English rules differs slightly in meaning from the irregular foreign plural. Thus 'indexes' usually applies to guides in books and 'indices' is usually used in mathematics. Some nouns have irregular plurals in that the plural form and the singular form are the same. These include 'sheep', 'grouse' (the game-bird) and 'salmon'. Some nouns have a regular plural and an irregular plural form. Thus 'brother' has the plural forms 'brothers' and 'brethren', although 'brethren' is now mainly used in a religious context and is archaic in general English.

irregular sentence *see* **major sentence**.

irregular verb
A verb that does not conform to the usual pattern of verbs in that some of its forms deviate from what one would expect if the pattern of regular verbs was being followed. There are four main forms of a **regular verb**—the INFINITIVE or base form, as in 'hint', 'halt', 'hate' and 'haul'; the third-person singular form, as 'hints', 'halts', 'hates' and 'hauls'; the -ING form or present participle, as 'hinting', halting', 'hating' and 'hauling'; the -ed form or 'past tense' or 'past participle', as 'hinted', halted', 'hated' and 'hauled.

Irregular verbs deviate in some way from that pattern, in particular from the pattern of adding -ed to the past tense and past participle. They fall into several categories.

One category concerns those that have the same form in the past tense and past participle forms as the infinitive and do not end in -ed, like regular verbs. These include:

infinitive	past tense	past participle
bet	bet	bet
burst	burst	burst

infinitive	past tense	past participle
cast	cast	cast
cost	cost	cost
cut	cut	cut
hit	hit	hit
hurt	hurt	hurt
let	let	let
put	put	put
run	run	run
set	set	set
shed	shed	shed
shut	shut	shut
slit	slit	slit
split	split	split
spread	spread	spread

Some irregular verbs have two past tenses and two past participles which are the same, as in:

infinitive	past tense	past participle
burn	burned, burnt	burned, burnt,
hang	hanged, hung,	hanged, hung
kneel	kneeled, knelt,	kneeled, knelt
lean	leaned, leant	learned, learnt
leap	leaped, leapt,	leaped, leapt
learn	learned, learnt	learned, learnt
light	lighted, lit	lighted, lit
smell	smelled, smelt	smelled, smelt
speed	speeded, sped	speeded, sped
spill	spilled, spilt	spilled, spilt
spoil	spoiled, spoilt	spoiled, spoilt

infinitive	past tense	past participle
wet	wetted, wet	wetted, wet

Some irregular verbs have past tenses that do not end in *-ed* and have the same form as the past participle. These include:

infinitive	past tense	past participle
become	became	became
bend	bent	bent
bleed	bled	bled
breed	bred	bred
build	built	built
cling	clung	clung
come	came	came
dig	dug	dug
feel	felt	felt
fight	fought	fought
find	found	found
flee	fled	fled
fling	flung	flung
get	got	got
grind	ground	ground
hear	heard	heard
hold	held	held
keep	kept	kept
lay	laid	laid
lead	led	led
leave	left	left
lend	lent	lent
lose	lost	lost
make	made	made

infinitive	*past tense*	*past participle*
mean	meant	meant
meet	met	met
pay	paid	paid
rend	rent	rent
say	said	said
seek	sought	sought
sell	sold	sold
send	sent	sent
shine	shone	shone
shoe	shod	shod
sit	sat	sat
sleep	slept	slept
slide	slid	slid
sling	slung	slung
slink	slunk	slunk
spend	spent	spent
spin	spun	spun
stand	stood	stood
stick	stuck	stuck
sting	stung	stung
strike	struck	struck
string	strung	strung
sweep	swept	swept
swing	swung	swung
teach	taught	taught
tell	told	told
think	thought	thought
understand	understood	understood
weep	wept	wept

infinitive	past tense	past participle
win	won	won
wring	wrung	wrung

Some irregular verbs have regular past tense forms but two possible past participles, one of which is regular. These include:

infinitive	past tense	past participle
mow	mowed	mowed, mown
prove	proved	proved, proven
sew	sewed	sewn, sewed
show	showed	showed, shown
sow	sowed	sowed, sown
swell	swelled	swelled, swollen

Some irregular verbs have past tenses and past participles that are different from each other and different from the infinitive. These include:

infinitive	past tense	past participle
arise	arose	arisen
awake	awoke	awoken
bear	bore	borne
begin	began	begun
bid	bade	bidden
bite	bit	bitten
blow	blew	blown
break	broke	broken
choose	chose	chosen
do	did	done
draw	drew	drawn
drink	drank	drunk

infinitive	*past tense*	*past participle*
drive	drove	driven
eat	ate	eaten
fall	fell	fallen
fly	flew	flown
forbear	forbore	forborne
forbid	forbade	forbidden
forgive	forgave	forgiven
forget	forgot	forgotten
forsake	forsook	forsaken
freeze	froze	frozen
forswear	forswore	forewarn
give	gave	given
go	went	gone
grow	grew	grown
hew	hewed	hewn
hide	hid	hidden
know	knew	known
lie	lay	lain
ride	rode	ridden
ring	rang	rung
saw	sawed	sawn
see	saw	seen
rise	rose	risen
shake	shook	shaken
shrink	shrank	shrunk
slay	slew	slain
speak	spoke	spoken
spring	sprang	sprung
steal	stole	stolen

infinitive	past tense	past participle
stink	stank	stunk
strew	strewed	strewn
stride	strode	stridden
strive	strove	striven
swear	swore	sworn
swim	swam	swum
take	took	taken
tear	tore	torn
throw	threw	thrown
tread	trod	trodden
wake	woken	woke
wear	wore	worn
write	written	wrote

-ise and -ize

These are both verb endings. In British English there are many verbs that can be spelt ending in either **-ise** or **-ize**, as 'computerise/ize', 'economise/ize', 'finalist/ize', 'hospitalise/ize', 'modernise/ize', 'organise/ize', 'realise/ize', 'theorise/ize'. There are a few verbs which cannot be spelt -ize. These include 'advertise', 'advise', 'comprise', 'despise', 'exercise', 'revise', 'supervise' and 'televise'.

-ish

A suffix indicating 'somewhat', as in baldish, biggish, smallish, youngish, and 'nationality', as in Spanish, Turkish and Polish.

-ism

A suffix indicating 'state, condition', as in absenteeism, alcoholism, fatalism, heroism and plagiarism, or indicating 'doctrine, movement, system, theory', as in Catholicism, Marxism and Thatcherism. It now also indicates 'discrimination', as in ageism, sexism, racism.

iso-
A prefix indicating 'equal', as in isobar, isotherm and isosceles.

-ist
A suffix indicating 'believer, supporter, practitioner', as in atheist, fascist, feminist and Methodist.

italic type
A sloping typeface that is used for a variety of purposes. It is used to differentiate a piece of text from the main text, which is usually in Roman type. For example, it is used sometimes for the titles of books, newspapers, magazines, plays, films, musical works and works of art, as in 'he is a regular reader of *The Times*', 'She reads *Private Eye*', 'Have you read *Animal Farm* by George Orwell', 'He has never seen a production of Shakespeare's *Othello*', 'We went to hear Handel's *Messiah*', '*Mona Lisa* is a famous painting'. Sometimes such titles are put in quotation marks rather than in italic.

Italic type is also sometimes used for the names of ships, trains, etc, as in 'the launch of *The Queen Elizabeth II*', 'She once sailed in *The Queen Mary*' and 'Their train was called *The Flying Scotsman*'.

Italic type is also used for the Latin names of plants and animals, as in 'of the genus *Lilium*', 'trees of the genus *Pyrus*', '*Panthera pardus*' and '*Canis lupus*'.

Italic type is sometimes used for foreign words that have been adopted into the English language but have never been fully integrated. Examples include *bête noire*, *raison d'être*, *inter alia* and *Weltschmerz*.

Italic type can also sometimes be used to draw attention to a particular word, phrase or passage, as in 'How do you pronounce *formidable*?', or to emphasize a word or phrase, as in 'Is he *still* in the same job?'

-ite

A suffix that can indicate 'believer, supporter, practitioner', as in Thatcherite and Trotskyite.

-itis

A suffix indicating 'illness or disease', as in bronchitis, hepatitis and meningitis.

its and it's

These are liable to be confused. **Its** is an adjective meaning 'belonging to it', as in 'The house has lost its charm' and 'The dog does not like its kennel'. **It's** means 'it is', as in 'Do you know if it's raining?' and 'It's not fair to expect her to do all the chores'.

-ize see -ise.

J

jargon

A technical or specialist language used among members of a particular profession or area. It is often used as a derogatory term to describe unnecessarily obscure or pretentious language, used within a profession, that is incomprehensible to members of the public who might come into contact with it and require to know what is being talked about. Jargon should be avoided in any document or situation involving lay people who have no specialist knowledge of the subject being referred to or of the language associated with it. Jargon in some professions easily becomes GODDLEDEGOOK.

journalese

A derogatory name for the style of writing and choice of vocabulary supposedly found in newspapers. It is usually the style of writing in tabloid newspapers, such as widespread use of clichés, sensational language and short sentences, that is meant by the term. See HEADLINE.

jussive

A type of clause or sentence that expresses a command, as in 'Do be quiet! I'm trying to study', 'Let's not bother going to the party. I'm too tired', 'Would you pass me that book' and 'Look at that everybody! The river has broken its banks'.

just

An adverb that indicates that something happened a short

time previously. In British English it is usually used with the perfect tense of the verb that it accompanies, as in 'I have just finished work', 'We have just decided to buy a new car', 'You've just missed the bus' and 'She's just passed her driving test'.

In American English, just usually accompanies the past tense of the verb, and some speakers of British English do also, especially in an informal context, as in 'I just saw a bad accident on the motorway', 'We just noticed that it's snowing' and 'He just left'.

Just has more than meaning. It can also mean 'only' and 'exactly'. In the sense of 'only', care should be taken to position it in the correct place in the sentence. For example, in the sentence 'He drank just two glasses of wine', it means that he drank only two glasses of wine, but in the sentence 'He just drank two glasses of wine' it means that he very recently drank two glasses of wine. To add to the confusion, although people may be careful about the positioning of just in formal writing they tend not to be in informal writing or speech. Thus someone could say in reply to the questions 'How much has he had to drink? Is he fit to drive?', 'He just had two glasses of wine', meaning that that was all he had drunk. In speech the meaning is usually obvious from intonation and context.

Just can also be used in the sense of 'only' in such sentences as 'Just Peter went on holiday with his parents. The other children stayed at home' and 'Just one coat was left. The rest were sold early on'. Again care should be taken to place just before the word it refers to in order to avoid ambiguity.

Just can also mean 'exactly', as in 'I see you have a food processor. That's just what I need' and 'Where did you find that cape? That's just what I've been looking for'.

K

kibbutzim

An example of an IRREGULAR PLURAL form. Most nouns in English form plurals by adding -s or -es to the singular form, as in 'book and books' and 'church and churches'. However several words of foreign origin which have been adopted into English but not fully integrated retain the plural form found in the foreign language. 'Kibbutz', meaning a communal settlement in Israel, is one such word. Of Hebrew origin, it retains the plural form kibbutzim. In some cases there is a growing tendency for foreign plurals to be anglicized, or to exist alongside an anglicized plural, as in 'thesauruses/thesauri', but this is not yet the case with kibbutzim.

kilo-

A prefix indicating 'a thousand', as in kilogram, kilohertz, kilolitre, kilometre and kilowatt.

-kin

A suffix that indicates 'a diminutive or smaller version', as in lambkin and mannikin.

kind

A noun that can cause grammatical problems. It is used to refer to a class of people or things. Since it is a COUNTABLE NOUN, it should take the plural form 'kinds' after words such as 'all' and 'many', as in 'He met all kinds of people when he was travelling round the world', 'We found all kinds of treasure when we were clearing out the attic' and 'We found all kinds of wild flower in the meadows'. A singular noun should follow 'kinds of', as in 'We found all kinds of treasure', but it is quite common for people to use a plural noun instead, as in 'We found all kinds of treasures'. This is best restricted to informal or spoken use.

'These' and 'those' are frequently found preceding **kind of**, as in 'She doesn't like these kind of cakes' and 'My mother used to make those kind of biscuits' but this is incorrect, and 'this' and 'that' should be used, as in 'I don't like that kind of joke' and 'My mother prefers this kind of holiday'.

The use of kind of to mean 'somewhat' or 'rather', as in 'I'm kind of hungry', 'She's kind of rude to him' and It's kind of cold in there', should be restricted to informal speech or dialect. This phrase is sometimes written 'kinda', as in 'We're kinda bored'.

Kind is also used as an adjective meaning 'caring' or 'generous', as in 'A kind old lady lent the children money to get a bus home', 'It was kind of you to let them borrow your car' and 'Children should be taught to be kind to animals'.

-kind

A suffix indicating 'a group of people', as in humankind, mankind, womankind.

kindly

A word that looks like an adverb but can be either an adverb or an adjective. As an adverb it means 'in a kind or caring manner' or 'generously', as in 'They treated us kindly during our stay', 'Her parents kindly treated us to a meal in a restaurant' and 'They very kindly offered us a lift'. The adverb kindly is also used in rather an ironic way when the user is annoyed, as in 'Would you kindly stop allowing your dog to foul the pavement'. It is also used in the phrase 'not to take kindly to', meaning 'to be unwilling to accept', as in 'The new pupil doesn't take kindly to discipline', 'He won't take kindly to being kept waiting' and 'The candidate was so confident that he is unlikely to take kindly to being rejected'.

Kindly is more common as an adjective and means 'kind, warm, friendly', as in 'a kindly old lady who was always helping her neighbours' and 'She gave the children a kindly smile'.

kneel

One of several verbs in English that have more than one past participle and past tense form. The past participle and past tense can both be either 'kneeled' or 'knelt', as in 'The child knelt in prayer', 'She kneeled before the altar' and 'She had knelt at her dying husband's bedside every night' and 'They had kneeled in supplication before the emperor but he spurned them'. Although both 'knelt' and 'kneeled' are acceptable forms in British English, 'knelt' is the more common form.

L

laid and lain

Words that are liable to be confused. **Laid** is the past tense and past participle of the verb 'lay', meaning 'to place or put', as in 'She laid the antique vase carefully on the table', 'He laid the new carpet tiles in the hall', 'They have laid the baby on a mat on the floor' and 'We have laid vinyl tiles on the kitchen floor'. **Lain** is the past participle of the verb 'lie', 'to rest in a horizontal position', as in 'Those letters have lain on his desk all week', 'The dead man had lain in the empty house for several days', and 'They had lain on the beach in the midday sun'.

language

The means by which human beings communicate using words, as in 'Children acquire language at different rates. Some speak much earlier than others'. Language can refer either to spoken or written communication. It can also refer to the variety of communication used by a particular nation or state, as in 'He visits France regularly but makes no attempt to understand the French language', 'He won't start to learn a foreign language until he goes to secondary school' and 'People in other parts of Europe tend to speak more languages than the British'. The language that a person speaks from birth is known as his/her 'first language' or 'mother tongue'. He/she is said to be a native speaker of this language.

Language can also be used to refer to the style and vocabulary of a piece of writing, as in 'The language of his novels is very poetic'.

Language can also apply to the particular style and variety of language that is used in a particular profession or among a particular group of people with some common interest, as in 'legal language', 'scientific language', 'technical language', etc. Such technical or specialist language is sometimes referred to rather pejoratively as JARGON or as 'legalese', 'medicalese', 'computerese', etc.

A person's own style of language with regard to vocabulary, structure, etc, is known as IDEOLECT, as in 'He is the son of academic parents and has rather a formal ideolect'.

The language of a region or community with regard to vocabulary, structure, grammar and pronunciation is known as DIALECT, as in 'the dialect of the Northeast of England', 'the dialects of the Southern states of the USA'.

last

A word that can be an adverb or an adjective. As an adjective it can give rise to ambiguity. It can mean 'coming after all others, final', as in 'He was the last runner to hit the finishing tape', 'That was the last novel he wrote before he died', 'He did not die until he was 90 but he wrote his last novel at the age of 40'. Ambiguity arises when last takes on other meanings. For example, it is frequently used as a synonym for 'latest', as in 'I really enjoyed his last novel and I'm looking forward to the next'. In this particular sentence it is clear that last means 'latest' not 'final' but this is not always the case. For example, in the sentence 'He was 60 when he directed his last film', it is not at all clear from the evidence of the sentence alone whether it is his 'final' or 'latest' film that is being referred to. Thus it is better to use either 'final' or 'latest' rather than 'last' in order to clarify the meaning.

Confusion can arise also between last, meaning 'final', and last, meaning 'preceding', as in 'I did not quite understand the last chapter'. On the evidence of the sentence alone, it is not clear whether last refers to the preceding chapter or to the final chapter. Again it is best to avoid ambiguity by using a synonym for last.

Yet more confusion can be caused with regard to last when it is used to refer to days of the week. It varies from person to person whether 'last Saturday' refers to the Saturday that has just gone or to the one before that. To some extent it depends which day of the week it is when the statement is made. To avoid ambiguity it is best to specify the date.

Last is also used as an adverb, as in 'They last saw their father when he was going to war', 'When the family go to the dentist my brother always wants to go in last' and 'If you are adding cream to the soup you add it last'. The adverbial use does not suffer from problems of ambiguity.

latest

An adjective that is liable to be confused with LAST. It can also mean 'most up-to-date', 'most fashionable', as in 'the very latest dresses from the Paris designers'. Latest is also found in this meaning in the phrase 'the very latest', as in 'she always dresses in the very latest'. It can also mean 'most late', the superlative of 'late', in the sense of 'far on in the day or night', as in 'The latest train which you can get from that station leaves at ten o' clock'. In this sense latest is also found in the phrase 'at the latest' and in the phrase 'at the very latest', meaning 'most late time', as in 'You must arrive at the station at ten o'clock at the latest' and 'The students' essays must be handed in by Friday at the very latest'.

lay and lie

These are liable to be confused. This is because **lay** as well as being a verb in its own right is also one of the principal parts of **lie**—the past tense, as in 'They lay on the beach in the sun', 'The books lay on the table gathering dust' and 'She lay on her bed and wept'.

Lay is a TRANSITIVE VERB meaning 'to place or put', as in 'She asked him to lay new tiles in the kitchen' and 'She had to lay down her shopping to open the door'. The principal parts of lay are 'lays' (third person singular present), as in 'She always lays the baby on the grass to play'; 'laying' (present participle), as in 'Laying her shopping down she put her key in the lock'; 'laid' (past participle and past tense), as in 'She laid the package on the table' and 'He had laid his car keys on the table and forgotten about them'.

Lie is an INTRANSITIVE VERB whose princiiplal parts are 'lies' (third person singular present), as in 'Their house lies to the north of the village'; 'lying' (present participle), as in 'Lying on the grass they looked up at the sky'; 'lay' (past tense), as in 'The climbers lay on the summit exhausted'; 'lain' (past participle), as in 'Those books have lain there for weeks'.

Lie has another totally unrelated meaning. It means 'to say or write something that is untrue', as in 'You didn't have to lie about your part in the affair'. The principal parts of the verb lie are 'lies' (third person singular present), as in 'lies about why he arrives home late from work'; 'lying' (present participle), as in 'Lying, he looked her straight in the face'; 'lied' (past participle and past tense), as in 'He lied to his employers about his qualifications' and 'she suddenly realized that he had lied all the time'.

lean
One of several verbs in English that have two forms of the past tense and the past participle, 'leaned' and 'leant', as in 'She leaned over the fence to talk to her neighbour', 'He leaned over his desk to catch the attention of his colleagues', 'They have leaned over backwards to help her' and 'She has leant down to pick something up and hurt her back'. The two forms are interchangeable.

leap
One of several verbs in English that have two forms of the past tense and past participle, 'leaped' and 'leapt', as in 'The children leaped around the park in high spirits', 'She leapt up in surprise when she heard the news', 'She had leaped over a high fence and broken her leg' and 'The child has leapt over the steam and run off'. The two forms are virtually interchangeable but 'leapt' is more common in British English.

learn
One of several verbs in English that have two forms of the past tense and past participle, 'learned' and 'learnt', as in 'They learned French at school', 'She learnt to ski in Austria', 'I think the boys have learned their lesson' and 'He had learnt to be

grateful for what he was given'. The forms are interchangeable. 'Learned' as a past tense or past participle should not be confused with 'learned', the adjective meaning 'erudite, well-read, intellectual', as in 'Students filled the lecture hall to listen to the learned professor' and 'The company publishes learned journals'. This adjective is pronounced with two syllables—*lernid*—whereas 'learned', the past tense and past participle, is pronounced as one syllable—*lernd*.

length mark

A mark used in phonetics in relation to a vowel to indicate that it is long. This can take the form of a 'macron', a small horizontal stroke placed above a letter, or a symbol resembling a colon placed after a vowel in the IPA pronunciation system.

-less

A suffix meaning 'without, lacking' added to nouns to form adjectives, as in characterless, clueless, expressionless, fearless, flawless, harmless, homeless, hopeless, passionless, toothless and useless. It can also mean 'without being able to be measured', as in ageless, countless, priceless and timeless.

less and fewer

Two words that are liable to be confused. See FEWER.

-let

A suffix indicating a diminutive or smaller form of something, as in booklet, coverlet, droplet, islet, piglet, starlet and streamlet.

letter-writing

This has become something of a dying art in view of the widespread use of the telephone. However, all of us from time to time have to write some form of letter and many of these are business letters. There are a few conventions in formal letters that should be observed.

One's own address, including one's postcode, should be placed at the right-hand side of the page. Each line of one's own address should be indented slightly below the one above and the date put below the last line of the address, as in:

> 23 Park Drive
> Raleigh
> Blackshire
> RA14 2TY
>
> 5 June 1993

Whether one puts a comma at the end of the various lines of the address is a matter of taste. It is becoming common in modern usage not to do so. Note that there should be no full stop after the postcode.

One's telephone number can either be placed between the postcode and the date or at the other side of the page on the same line as the first line of the address.

If one is writing a business letter one should also put the address of the person to whom one is writing. It should be placed at the other side of the page below one's own address and the lines of this should be placed directly below each other without being indented, as in:

23, Park Drive
Raleigh
Blackshire
RA 14 2TY

5 June 1993

The Manager Eastlands Bank
33 West Street
Northlands
Blackshire
NR15 3RJ

With regard to deciding how to address the person to whom one is writing it is best to find out his/her name. Having done so then one can start the letter off, as in:

Dear Mr White,

If one is writing to a woman the situation is slightly more problematic. Formerly it was considered acceptable to address the person written to as 'Miss' if one knew her to be unmarried or as 'Mrs' if one knew her to be married. If one did not know her marital status one could either use 'Miss' or use the 'Madam' convention. In modern usage 'Ms' is the acceptable term if one does not know the marital status of the woman to whom one is writing. Many people prefer to use this designation even if they do know the person's marital status and many women prefer to be addressed in this way. On the other hand, some women, especially older women, do not like the 'Ms' designation.

In modern usage some people prefer to put the first name

and surname of the relevant person instead of the surname preceded by Mr, etc, as in:

> Dear John White,

The above style of address is considered rather informal by some people.

If it is not easy to ascertain the name of the person to whom one wishes to write then it is perfectly acceptable to address him/her in terms of their position or job, as in:

> Dear manager,
> Dear Personnel Manager,
> Dear Area Manager,

In formal letters it is also acceptable to use 'Sir' or 'Madam', as in:

> Dear Sir,
> Dear Madam,
> Dear Sir/Madam,

Obviously the above style of address is used in cases where one does not know the sex of the person to whom one is writing.

In ending a formal letter it was traditionally the custom to write 'Yours faithfully' before one's signature, if one had addressed the person written to as 'Dear sir' or 'Dear madam', as in:

> Yours faithfully,
> Jane Black

It was also the custom to end the letter with 'Yours sincerely' if the letter was either informal in nature or a formal letter which began with 'Dear Mr White' etc, as in:

> Yours sincerely,
> Mary Brown

In modern usage it is now considered acceptable to end a letter with 'Yours sincerely' even if one has begun it with 'Dear sir', etc. These days 'Yours faithfully' is considered to be exceptionally formal.

It is common to end even business letters with 'Kind regards', especially if the person written to is known to one.

On the envelope the lines can be indented or not, according to taste. Each line, except the last one, can have a comma after or not. However, in modern usage there is an increasing tendency to punctuate as little as possible and the commas are frequently omitted, as in:

> Ms Mary Brown
> 29 Lower Forth Street
> Redwood
> Blackshire
> RD16 5YP

The same comments on Mrs, Miss and Ms apply to envelopes as apply to the opening greeting in letters. *See above.* Anything that can be done to make the address as clear as possible should be done. It is important always to put the postcode in the address as failure to do so slows down delivery of the letter. It is also advisable to highlight the town one is sending the letter to, either by putting it in capital letters, or by underlining it, as in:

Mr James Green
45 Park Avenue
BOSTON
Blackshire
BT16 6GH

In modern usage it is becoming increasingly common to write the full name of the person written to on the envelope, as in:

James Black
36 High Street
BLANKTON
Blankshire
BL13 9TZ

It is considered formal or old-fashioned to use 'Esq.', usually spelt with a full stop at the end and preceded by a comma. If used, 'Esq.' should be placed after the mans's name and there should be no accompanying 'Mr', as in:

John Brown, Esq
43 Queen Street
Whiteoaks
Blankshire
WH12 TY

lexicography
The art and practice of defining words, selecting them and arranging them in dictionaries and glossaries.

licence and license
These are liable to be confused. **Licence** is a noun referring

to 'a document indicating that official permission or authorization has been given to do something', as in 'He does not have a current driving licence', 'You need a trading licence to sell goods there' and 'The pub owner lost his licence'. Licence also means 'too great freedom, disregard for rules of behaviour, social acceptability, morals, etc', as in 'The organizers of the concert objected to the licence shown by the young people in their dress'. In this sense the word licence is usually used in formal situations.

License is a verb meaning 'to give a licence to, to give official permission or authorization to', as in 'He is licensed to sell alcohol', 'She is not licensed to sell goods in the market' and 'The restaurant is not licensed but you can bring your own wine'. Licence is often misspelt as license.

The above comments refer to British English. In American English license is used for both the noun and the verb.

lie see **lay**.

ligature
A printed character combining two letters in one, as in æ and œ. It is sometimes called a DIGRAPH.

-like
A suffix indicating similarity, as in childlike, cowlike, dreamlike, ladylike, lifelike and warlike.

-ling
A suffix indicating a diminutive or smaller version of something, as in duckling, gosling and nestling.

-logue

A suffix derived from Greek meaning 'indicating 'conversation, discussion', as in dialogue, epilogue, monologue, prologue and travelogue.

limerick

A humorous five-lined piece of light verse, with the first two lines rhyming with each other, the third and fourth lines rhyming with each other, and the fifth line rhyming with the first line. Usually there are three stressed beats in the first, second and fifth lines and two stressed beats on the third and fourth lines. Traditionally the name of a place is mentioned in the first line and may be repeated in the last line. Edward Lear made the form popular in the nineteenth century. Limerick is a town in Ireland but the name of the verse is probably derived from a Victorian custom of singing nonsense songs at parties where 'Will you come up to Limerick' was a common refrain. An example is:

> There once was a man from Nantucket
> Who kept all his cash in a bucket;
>> But his daughter named Nan
>> Ran away with a man,
> And as for the bucket, Nantucket.

lingua franca

A language defined as 'a language adopted as a common language by speakers whose mother tongues or native languages are different'. This enables people to have a common medium of communication for various purposes, such as trading. Examples include Swahili in East Africa, Hausa in West Africa and

Tok Pisin in Papua New Guinea. The term historically referred to 'a language that was a mixture of Italian, French, Greek, Spanish and Arabic, used for trading and military purposes.'

linguistics

The systematic, scientific study of language. It describes language and seeks to establish general principles rather than to prescribe rules of correctness.

line-break

The division of a word at the end of a line for space purposes. This is marked by a HYPHEN.

linking adverbs and linking adverbials

Words and phrases that indicate some kind of connection between one clause or sentence and another. Examples include 'however', as in 'The award had no effect on their financial situation. It did, however, have a marked effect on their morale'; 'moreover', as in 'He is an unruly pupil. Moreover, he is a bad influence on the other pupils'; 'then again', as in 'She does not have very good qualifications. Then again, most of the other candidates have even fewer'; 'in the meantime', as in 'We will not know the planning committee's decision until next week. In the meantime we can only hope'; 'instead', as in 'I thought he would have reigned. Instead he seems determined to stay'.

linking verb

A verb that 'links' a subject with its complement. Unlike other verbs, linking verbs do not denote an action but indicate a state. Examples of linking verbs include 'He is a fool', 'She appears calm', 'He appeared a sensible man', 'You seemed to become anxious', 'They became Buddhists', 'The child feels unwell', 'It is getting rather warm', 'It is growing colder', 'You look well', 'She remained loyal to her friend', 'She lived in America but remained a British citizen' and 'You seem thoughtful' and 'She seems a nice person'. Linking verbs are also called **copula** or **copular verbs**.

literary criticism

The formal study, discussion and evaluation of a literary work, as in 'The students who are studying literary criticism have been asked to write a critical analysis of *Ulysses* by James Joyce.'

litotes

A kind of understatement in which a statement is conveyed by contradicting or denying its opposite, as in 'It will be no easy task to look after their children for a week' (meaning that it will be a difficult task), 'She's not exactly communicative' (meaning she is silent or reserved).

loanword

A word that has been taken into one language from another. From the point of view of the language taking the word in, the word is known as a BORROWING. Some loanwords become naturalized or fully integrated into the language and have a pronunciation and spelling reflecting the conventions of the language which has borrowed it. Other loanwords retain the spelling and pronunciation of the language from which they have been borrowed. These include 'Gastarbeiter', borrowed from German and meaning 'a foreign worker'.

localism

A word or expression the use of which is restricted to a particular place or area. The area in question can be quite small, unlike DIALECT words or 'regionalism'.

lower-case letter

The opposite of CAPITAL LETTER. It is also known informally as 'small letter'. Lower-case letters are used for most words in the language. It is capital letters that are exceptional in their use.

-ly

A common adverbial ending. See ADVERBS.

M

macro-
A prefix derived from the Greek meaning 'large in size or scope', as in macrobiotic, macrocosm, macroeconomics, macromolecular and macrostructure.

macron see **length mark**.

main clause
The principal clause in a sentence on which any SUBORDINATE CLAUSES depend for their sense. The main clause can stand alone and make some sense but the subordinate clauses cannot. In the sentence 'I left early because I wanted to catch the 6 o'clock train', 'I left early' is the principal clause and 'because I wanted to catch the 6 o'clock train' is the subordinate clause. In the sentence 'When we saw the strange man we were afraid', the main clause is 'we were afraid' and the subordinate clause is 'when we saw the strange man'. In the sentence 'Because it was late we decided to start out for home as soon as we could', the main clause is 'we decided to start out for home' and the subordinate clauses are 'because it was late' and 'as soon as we could'. A main clause can also be known as a **principal clause** or an INDEPENDENT CLAUSE.

mal-

A prefix derived from French meaning 'bad, unpleasant', as in malodorous, or 'imperfect, faulty', as in malabsorption, maladjusted, maladministration, malformation, malfunctioning, malnutrition, malpractice and maltreatment.

malapropism

The incorrect use of a word, often through confusion with a similar-sounding word. It often arises from someone's attempt to impress someone else with a knowledge of long words or of technical language. Examples include 'The doctor says the old man is not in possession of all his facilities'. Here 'facilities' has been wrongly used instead of 'faculties'. Another example is 'My friend lives in a computer belt'. Here 'computer' has been wrongly used instead of 'commuter'. Another example is 'Her husband's had a vivisection'. Here 'vivisection' has been used instead of 'vasectomy'. 'Ah! It's wonderful to be on terracotta again. I hate sailing'. Here 'terracotta' has been wrongly used instead of 'terra firma'. The effect of malapropism is often humorous. Sometimes people use it deliberately for a comic effect, as in 'He was under the affluence of incahol'.

Malapropism is called after Mrs Malaprop, a character in a play called *The Rivals* (1775), a comedy by R. B. Sheridan. Her name is derived from the French *mal à propos*, 'not apposite, inappropriate'. Some of her malapropisms in the play include 'She's as headstrong as an allegory on the banks of the Nile'. She has used 'allegory' wrongly instead of 'alligator'. Another of Mrs Malapropism's malapropisms is 'Illiterate him quite from your mind'. Here she has used 'illiterate' wrongly instead of 'obliterate'.

major sentence

A sentence that contains at least one SUBJECT and a FINITE VERB, as in 'We are going' and 'They won'. They frequently have more elements than this, as in 'They bought a car', 'We lost the match', 'They arrived yesterday' and 'We are going away next week'. They are sometimes described as **regular** because they divide into certain structural patterns: a subject, finite verb, adverb or adverbial clause, etc. The opposite of a major sentence is called a **minor sentence**, **irregular sentence** or **fragmentary sentence**. These include interjections such as 'Ouch!' and 'How terrible'; formula expressions, such as 'Good morning' and 'Well done'; and short forms of longer expressions, as in 'Traffic diverted', 'Shop closed', 'No dogs' and 'Flooding ahead'. Such short forms could be rephrased to become major sentences, as in 'Traffic has been diverted because of roadworks', 'The shop is closed on Sundays', 'The owner does not allow dogs in her shop' and 'There was flooding ahead on the motorway'.

-man

A suffix used with nouns to form nouns indicating someone's job, as in barman, chairman, clergyman, coalman, fireman, policeman, postman, salesman.

In modern usage, when attempts are being made to remove sexism from the language, alternatives have been sought for any words ending in -man. Formerly, words ending in -man were often used whether or not the person referred to was definitely known to be a man. Different ways have been found to avoid the sexism of -man. 'Salesman' has been changed in many cases to 'salesperson', 'chairman' often becomes 'chairperson' or 'chair'. Similarly, 'fireman' has become 'fire-fighter' and 'policeman' frequently becomes 'police officer'. *See* -PER-SON.

-mania
A suffix indicating abnormal or obsessional behaviour, as in kleptomania, nymphomania and pyromania.

manner, adverbs of *see* **adverb**.

manner, adverbial clause of *see* **adverbial clause**.

masculine
In grammatical terms, one of the GENDERS that nouns are divided into. Nouns in the masculine gender include words that obviously belong to the male sex, as in 'man', 'boy', 'king', 'prince' 'bridegroom', 'schoolboy' and 'salesman'. Many words now considered to be of DUAL GENDER formerly were assumed to be masculine. These include such words as 'author', 'sculptor' and 'engineer'. Gender also applies to personal pronouns, and the third personal singular pronoun masculine is 'he' (subject), 'him' (object) and 'his' (possessive). For further information *see* HE; SHE.

mass noun the same as **uncountable noun**.

-mate
A suffix referring to 'someone who shares something with someone', as in bedmate, classmate, room-mate, schoolmate, shipmate, team-mate and workmate.

mega-
A prefix derived from Greek meaning 'very large', as in megabid, megabucks, megaproduction and megastar. Many words using mega- in this way are modern and many are also informal or slang. In technical language mega- means 'a million times bigger than the unit to which it is attached, as in megabyte, megacycle, megahertz and megawatt.

meiosis
A figure of speech using understatement to emphasize the size or importance of something, as in 'He's a decent enough bloke' and 'He's rather a decent tennis player'.

melted and molten
Words that are liable to be confused. **Melted** is the past tense and past participle of the verb 'to melt', as in 'The chocolate melted in the heat' and 'The ice cream had melted by the time they got home'. Melted is also used as an adjective, as in 'melted chocolate'. **Molten** is used only as an adjective but it is not synonymous with melted. It means 'melted or made liquid at high temperatures', as in 'molten lava' and 'molten metal'.

meta-
A prefix derived from Greek indicating 'alteration or transformation', as in metamorphosis, metaphor and metaphysics.

metaphor
A figure of speech that compares two things by saying that one thing is another, as in 'He was a lion in the fight' (meaning that

he was as brave as a lion), 'She is a mouse whenever he is present' (meaning that she is very timid), 'He is a giant among men' (meaning that he is a great man), 'She was a shining light to us all' (meaning she was a source of inspiration) and 'Life was not a bed of roses' (meaning life was not easy and enjoyable). By extension, metaphor refers to a word or phrase used in a sentence where it does not have a literal meaning, as in 'a butter mountain', 'a wine lake', 'My colleague is a snake in the grass', 'She always sits on the fence at committee meetings', They walked home with leaden feet' and 'He was rooted to the spot when he saw the man with the gun'. See MIXED META-PHOR and SIMILE.

-meter

A suffix indicating 'a measuring instrument', as in altimeter, barometer, pedometer, calorimeter, speedometer, thermometer.

metonym

A figure of speech in which a word or expression is used to indicate something with which it has a close relationship, as in 'The position of the Crown is more uncertain than it was formerly' (meaning that the position of the monarchy is not as stable as it once was), 'The City is nervously awaiting the announcement of this month's trade figures' (meaning that the people who work in London's financial sector are nervously awaiting the announcement of this month's trade figures) and 'The Kremlin began to adopt a more enlightened approach to foreign visitors' (meaning that the Russian government began to adopt a more enlightened approach to foreign visitors), 'The White House has yet to comment on the proposal' (meaning that the President of the United States has yet to reply to the proposal).

-metre

A suffix indicating 'meter, the unit of length', as in centimetre, kilometre and millimetre.

micro-

A prefix derived from Greek meaning 'very small', as in microbiology, microfiche, microfilm, microscope, microsurgery.

milli-

A prefix derived from Latin meaning 'thousand', as in millisecond, millennium.

mini-

A prefix derived from Latin meaning 'very small, least', as in minimum, minimal, and miniature. Mini- is frequently used to form modern words, as in minibus, minicab, mini-computer, mini-cruise, mini-golf, mini-market and miniskirt. Modern words beginning with mini- can be spelt either with a hyphen or without.

minor sentence *see* **major sentence**.

mis-

A prefix indicating 'badly, wrongly', as in misbehave, miscalculate, misdirect, mishandle, mishear, misjudge, mismanage, mispronounce, misspell, mistreat, mistrust, misunderstanding and misuse.

misrelated participle *see* **dangling participle**.

mixed metaphor

The situation that occurs when unrelated METAPHORS are put in the same sentence. Examples include 'She sailed into the room with both guns blazing'. Here the use of the word 'sail' belongs to nautical metaphors but the 'guns blazing' belongs to cowboy or Wild West metaphors. Another example is 'The company's new flagship did not get off the ground'. Here 'flagship' is a nautical term while 'get off the ground' refers to an aircraft taking off. Another example is 'They were caught red-handed with their trousers down'. Here 'caught red-handed' is a metaphorical reference to a murderer caught with blood on his/her hands but 'caught with one's trousers down' is either a reference to the embarrassing experience of being caught unawares in the toilet or else caught in an embarrassing sexual situation.

modal verb

A type of AUXILIARY VERB that 'helps' the main verb to express a range of meanings including, for example, such meanings as possibility, probability, wants, wishes, necessity, permission, suggestions, etc. The main modal verbs are 'can', 'could'; 'may', 'might'; 'will', 'would'; 'shall', 'should'; 'must'. Modal verbs have only one form. They have no -s form in the third person singular, no infinitive and no participles. Examples of modal verbs include 'He cannot read and write', 'She could go if she wanted to' (expressing ability); 'You can have another biscuit', 'You may answer the question' (expressing permission); 'We may see her on the way to the station', 'We might get there by nightfall' (expressing possibility); 'Will you have some wine?', 'Would you take a seat?' (expressing an offer or invitation); 'We should arrive by dawn', 'That must be a record' (expressing probability and certainty); 'You may prefer to wait', 'You might like to leave instructions' (expressing suggestion); 'Can you find the time to phone him for me?', 'Could you give him a message?' (expressing instructions and requests); 'They must leave at once', 'We must get there on time' (expressing necessity).

modifier

A word, or group of words, that 'modifies' or affects the meaning of another word in some way, usually by adding more information about it. Modifiers are frequently used with nouns. They can be adjectives, as in 'He works in the *main* building' and 'They need a *larger* house'. Modifiers of nouns can be nouns themselves, as in 'the *theatre* profession', 'the *publishing* industry' and '*singing* tuition'. They can also be place names, as in 'the *Edinburgh* train', 'a *Paris* café' and 'the *London* underground', or adverbs of place and direction, as in 'a *downstairs* cloakroom' and 'an *upstairs* sitting room.

Adverbs, adjectives and pronouns can be accompanied by modifiers. Examples of modifiers with adverbs include 'walking *amazingly* quickly' and 'stopping *incredibly* abruptly'. Examples of modifiers with adjectives include 'a *really* warm day' and 'a *deliriously* happy child'. Examples of modifiers with pronouns include '*almost* no one there' and '*practically* everyone present'.

The examples given above are all premodifiers. See *also* POSTMODIFIER.

molten *see* **melted**.

-monger

A suffix derived from Old English meaning 'dealer, trader', as in fishmonger and ironmonger. As well as being used for occupations in which people sell things, it is used for people who 'trade' in less tangible things, as in gossipmonger, rumourmonger, scaremonger and warmonger.

mono-

A prefix derived from Greek meaning 'one, single', as in monochrome, monocracy, monogamy, monologue, monoplane, monosyllabic and monoxide.

months of the year

These are spelt with initial capital letters, as in January, February, March, April, May, June, July, August, September, October, November and December.

mood

One of the categories into which verbs are divided. The verb moods are indicative, imperative and subjunctive. The **indicative** makes a statement, as in 'He lives in France', 'They have two children' and 'It's starting to rain'. The **imperative** is used for giving orders or making requests, as in 'Shut that door!', 'Sit quietly until the teacher arrives' and 'Please bring me some coffee'. The **subjunctive** was originally a term in Latin grammar and expressed a wish, supposition, doubt, improbability or other non-factual statement. It is used in English for hypothetical statements and certain formal 'that' clauses, as in 'If I were you I would have nothing to do with it', 'If you were to go now you would arrive on time', 'Someone suggested that we ask for more money' and 'It was his solicitor who suggested that he sue the firm'. The word 'mood' arose because it was said to indicate the verb's attitude or viewpoint.

more

An adverb that is added to some adjectives to make the comparative form (see COMPARISON OF ADJECTIVES). In general it is the longer adjectives that have more as part of their comparative form, as in 'more abundant', 'more beautiful', 'more catastrophic', 'more dangerous', 'more elegant', 'more frantic', 'more graceful', 'more handsome', 'more intelligent', 'more luxurious', 'more manageable', 'more opulent', 'more precious', 'more ravishing', 'more satisfactory', 'more talented', 'more unusual', 'more valuable'. Examples of adverbs with more in their comparative form include 'more elegantly', 'more gracefully', 'more energetically', 'more dangerously' and 'more determinedly'.

most

An adverb added to some adjectives and adverbs to make the superlative form. In general it is the longer adjectives that have most as part of their superlative form, as in 'most abundant', 'most beautiful', 'most catastrophic', 'most dangerous', 'most elegant', 'most frantic', 'most graceful', 'most handsome', 'most intelligent', 'most luxurious', 'most manageable', 'most noteworthy', 'most opulent', 'most precious', most ravishing', 'most satisfactory', 'most talented', 'most unusual', 'most valuable'. Examples of adverbs with most in their superlative form include 'most elegantly', 'most gracefully', 'most energetically', 'most dangerously' and 'most determinedly'.

mother tongue

The language that one first learns, the language of which one is a 'native speaker'. It means the same as 'native tongue'.

ms, miss and **miss** *see* LETTER-WRITING.

mow

A verb that has two possible past participles—'mowed' and 'mown'—as in 'He has not yet mowed the grass' and 'We have mown the grass several times this summer'. The two participles are interchangeable. Only **mowed**, however, can be used as the past tense, as in 'They mowed the grass yesterday' and 'If they mowed the grass more often the garden would be tidier'. **Mown** can also be an adjective, as in 'the smell of freshly mown hay'.

multi-

A prefix derived from Latin meaning 'many', as in multiply, multitude and multitudinous. Multi- is frequently used to form new modern words, as in multi-married, multi-media, multi-publicized, multi-purpose, multi-storey, multi-talented and multi-travelled.

multi-sentence

A sentence with more than one clause, as in 'She tripped over a rock and broke her ankle' and 'She was afraid when she saw the strange man'.

N

-naut

A suffix derived from Greek 'sailor' and meaning 'navigator', as in astronaut and cosmonaut.

negative sentence

A sentence that is the opposite of a **positive sentence**. 'She has a dog' is an example of a positive sentence. 'She does not have a dog' is an example of a negative sentence. The negative concept is expressed by an AUXILIARY VERB accompanied by 'not' or 'n't'. Other words used in negative sentences include 'never', 'nothing' and 'by no means', as in 'She has never been here' and 'We heard nothing'.

neither

An adjective or a pronoun that takes a singular verb, as in 'Neither parent will come' and 'Neither of them wishes to come'. In the **neither ... nor** construction, a singular verb is used if both parts of the construction are singular, as in 'Neither Jane nor Mary was present'. If both parts are plural the verb is plural, as in 'Neither their parents nor their grandparents are willing to look after them'. If the construction involves a mixture of singular and plural, the verb traditionally agrees with the subject that is nearest it, as in 'Neither her mother nor her grandparents are going to come' and 'Neither her grandparents nor her mother is going to come'. If pronouns are used, the nearer one governs the verb as in 'Neither they nor he is at fault' and 'Neither he nor they are at fault'.

neologism
A word that has been newly coined or newly introduced into the language, as 'camcorder', 'Jacuzzi' and 'karaoke'.

neuro-
A prefix derived from Greek meaning 'nerve', as in neuritis, neurology, neuron and neurosurgery.

neuter
One of the grammatical GENDERS. The other two grammatical genders are MASCULINE and FEMININE. Inanimate objects are members of the neuter gender. Examples include 'table', 'desk', 'garden', 'spade', 'flower' and 'bottle'.

nominal clause see noun clause.

non-finite clause
A clause which contains a NON-FINITE VERB. Thus in the sentence 'He works hard to earn a living', 'to earn a living' is a non-finite clause since 'to earn' is an infinitive and so a non-finite verb. Similarly in the sentence 'Getting there was a problem', 'getting there' is a non-finite clause, 'getting' being a present participle and so a non-finite verb.

non-finite verb
A verb that shows no variation in tense and has no subject. The non-finite verb forms include the infinitive form, as in 'go',

the present participle and gerund, as in 'going', and the past participle, as in 'gone'.

non-gradable *see* **gradable**.

noun
The name of something or someone. Thus 'anchor', 'baker', 'cat', 'elephant', 'foot', 'gate', 'lake', 'pear', 'shoe', 'trunk' and 'wallet' are all nouns. There are various categories of nouns. *See* ABSTRACT NOUN, COMMON NOUN, CONCRETE NOUN, COUNTABLE NOUN, PROPER NOUN and UNCOUNTABLE NOUN.

noun clause
A SUBORDINATE CLAUSE that performs a function in a sentence similar to a noun or noun phrase. It can act as the subject, object or complement of a MAIN CLAUSE. In the sentence 'Where he goes is his own business', 'where he goes' is a noun clause. In the sentence 'They asked why he objected', 'why he objected' is a noun clause. A noun clause is also known as a **nominal clause**.

noun phrase
A group of words containing a noun as its main word and functioning like a noun in a sentence. Thus it can function as the SUBJECT, OBJECT or COMPLEMENT of a sentence. In the sentence 'The large black dog bit him', 'the large black dog' is a noun phrase, and in the sentence 'They bought a house with a garden', 'with a garden' is a noun phrase. In the sentence 'She is a complete fool', 'a complete fool' is a noun phrase.

number
In grammar this is a classification consisting of 'singular' and

'plural'. Thus the number of the pronoun 'they' is 'plural' and the number of the verb 'carries' is singular. See NUMBER AGREEMENT.

number agreement or concord

The agreement of grammatical units in terms of NUMBER. Thus a singular subject is followed by a singular verb, as in 'The girl likes flowers', 'He hates work' and 'She was carrying a suitcase'. Similarly a plural subject should be followed by a plural verb, as in 'They have many problems', 'The men work hard' and 'The girls are training hard'.

numbers

These can be written in either figures or words. It is largely a matter of taste which method is adopted. As long as the method is consistent it does not really matter. Some establishments, such as a publishing house or a newspaper office, will have a house style. For example, some of them prefer to have numbers up to 10 written in words, as in 'They have two boys and three girls'. If this system is adopted, guidance should be sought as to whether a mixture of figures and words in the same sentence is acceptable, as in 'We have 12 cups but only six saucers', or whether the rule should be broken in such situations as 'We have twelve cups but only six saucers'.

numeral

A word for 'number', as in 'print all the numerals in bold type'. Numeral is often used to refer to 'one, two, three, etc' in grammar since NUMBER is used to refer to the singular/plural category.

O

object

The part of a sentence that is acted upon or is affected by the verb. It usually follows the verb to which it relates. There are two forms of object—the DIRECT OBJECT and INDIRECT OBJECT. A direct object can be a noun, and in the sentence 'The girl hit the ball', 'ball' is a noun and the object. In the sentence 'They bought a house', 'house' is a noun and the object. In the sentence 'They made an error', 'error' is a noun and the object. A direct object can be a noun phrase, and in the sentence 'He has bought a large house', 'a large house' is a noun phrase and the object. In the sentence 'She loves the little girl', 'the little girl' is a noun phrase and the object. In the sentence 'They both wear black clothes', 'black clothes' is a noun phrase and the object'. A direct object can be a noun clause, and in the sentence 'I know what he means', 'what he means' is a noun phrase and the object. In the sentence 'He denied that he had been involved', 'that he had been involved' is a noun phrase and the object. In the sentence 'I asked when he would return', 'when he would return' is a noun phrase and the object. A direct object can also be a pronoun, and in the sentence 'She hit him', 'him' is a pronoun and the object. In the sentence 'They had a car but they sold it', 'it' is a pronoun and the object. In the sentence 'She loves them', 'them' is a pronoun and the object.

objective case

The case expressing the OBJECT. In Latin it is known as the AC-CUSATIVE case.

oblique

A diagonal mark (/) that has various uses. Its principal use is to show alternatives, as in 'he/she', 'Dear Sir/Madam', 'two/three-room flat' and 'the budget for 1993/4'. The oblique is used in some abbreviations, as in 'c/o Smith' (meaning 'care of Smith'). The word 'per' is usually shown by means of an oblique, as in 60km/h (60 kilometres per hour).

officialese

A derogatory term for the vocabulary and style of writing often found in official reports and documents and thought of as being pretentious and difficult to understand. It is usually considered to be the prime example of GOBBLEDEGOOK.

-oholic see **-aholic**.

-ology

A suffix derived from Greek indicating 'study of', as in biology, geology and technology.

omni-

A prefix derived from Latin indicating 'all', as in omnipotent and omnivorous.

onomatopoeia

A figure of speech that uses words whose sound suggests their meaning, as in 'The sausages sizzled in the pan', 'The fire crackled in the grate' and 'The water gurgled in the pipes'.

ordinal numbers
The numbers 'first', 'second', 'third', etc, as opposed to CARDINAL NUMBERS, which are 'one', 'two', 'three', etc.

orthographic
A term that refers to spelling, as in 'words which give rise to orthographic problems'.

orthography
The study or science of how words are spelt, as in 'make a survey of the orthography and the pronunciation of Scandinavian languages'.

-osis
A suffix derived from Greek indicating either 'a disease', as in cirrhosis and thrombosis, or a de veloment, as in metamorphosis.

oxymoron
A figure of speech that is based on the linking of incongruous or contradictory words, as in 'and honour rooted in dishonour stood' (Tennyson) and 'the wisest fool in Christendom'.

P

paragraph

A subdivision of a piece of prose. Many people find it difficult to divide their work into paragraphs. Learning to do so can be difficult but it is an area of style that improves with practice.

A paragraph should deal with one particular theme or point of the writer's writing or argument. When that has been dealt with, a new paragraph should be started. However, there are other considerations to be taken into account. If the paragraph is very long it can appear offputting visually to the would-be reader and can be difficult to make one's way through. In such cases it is best to subdivide themes and shorten paragraphs. On the other hand, it is best not to make all one's paragraphs too short as this can create a disjointed effect. It is best to try to aim for a mixture of lengths to create some variety.

Traditionally it was frowned upon to have a one-sentence paragraph but there are no hard and fast rules about this. Usually it takes more than one sentence to develop the theme of the paragraph, unless one is a tabloid journalist or copywriter for an advertising firm, and it is best to avoid long, complex sentences.

The opening paragraph of a piece of writing should introduce the topic about which one is writing. The closing paragraph should sum up what one has been writing about. New paragraphs begin on new lines and they are usually indented from the margin. In the case of dialogue in a work of fiction, each speaker's utterance usually begins on a new line for the clarification of the reader.

parenthesis see **brackets**.

participle
A part of speech, so called because, although a verb, it has the character both of verb and adjective and is also used in the formation of some compound tenses. See also -ING WORDS and PAST PARTICIPLE.

part of speech
Each of the categories (e.g. verb, noun, adjective, etc) into which words are divided according to their grammatical and semantic functions.

passive voice
The voice of a verb whereby the subject is the recipient of the action of the verb. Thus, in the sentence 'Mary was kicked by her brother', 'Mary' is the receiver of the 'kick' and so 'kick' is in the passive voice. Had it been in the active voice it would have been 'Her brother kicked Mary'. Thus 'the brother' is the subject and not the receiver of the action.

past participle
This is formed by adding -ed or -d to the base words of regular verbs, as in 'acted', ' alluded', 'boarded', 'dashed', 'flouted', 'handed', 'loathed', 'tended' and 'wanted', or in various other ways for IRREGULAR VERBS.

past tense

This TENSE of a verb is formed by adding -*ed* or -*d* to the base form of the verb in regular verbs, as in 'added', 'crashed', 'graded', 'smiled', 'rested' and 'yielded', and in various ways for IRREGULAR VERBS.

perfect tense *see* **tense**.

period *see* **full stop**.

personification

A form of METAPHOR that represents an inanimate object or abstract notion as possessing the attributes of a person. For example, Uncle Sam is a personification of the United States of America, while John Bull is a personfication of England.

personal pronoun

A pronoun that is used to refer back to someone or something that has already been mentioned. The personal pronouns are divided into subject pronouns, object pronouns and possessive pronouns. They are also categorized according to 'person'. See FIRST PERSON, SECOND PERSON and THIRD PERSON.

philology

The science, especially comparative, of languages and their history and structure.

phonetics

The science connected with pronunciation and the representation of speech sounds.

phrasal verb
A usually simple verb that combines with a preposition or adverb, or both, to convey a meaning more than the sum of its parts, e.g. to phase out, to come out, to look forward to.

phrase
Two or more words, usually not containing a FINITE VERB, that form a complete expression by themselves or constitute a portion of a sentence.

plural noun
The form of a noun referring to 'more than one' and contrasted with a SINGULAR NOUN. Singular nouns form plural forms in different ways. Most singular nouns add s, as in 'bat/bats', 'monkey/monkeys', 'table/tables', 'umbrella/umbrellas', or add es, as in 'church/churches' or 'torch/torches'. Singular nouns ending in a consonant followed by y add ies, as in 'fairy/fairies' and 'story/stories'. Some plural forms are formed irregularly (see IRREGULAR PLURALS). Some nouns are encountered in their plural form only. These include scissors, trousers and vermin.

point see **full stop**.

positive sentence see **negative sentence**.

possessive apostrophe see **apostrophe**[2].

possessive pronoun see **personal pronoun; first person; second person** and **third person**.

postmodifier
A MODIFIER that comes after the main word of a NOUN PHRASE, as in 'of stone' in 'tablets of stone'.

predicate

All the parts of a clause or sentence that are not contained in
the subject. Thus in the sentence 'The little girl was exhausted
and hungry', 'exhausted and hungry' is the predicate. Similarly,
in the sentence 'The tired old man slept like a top', 'slept like a
top' is the predicate.

predicative adjective

An adjective that helps to form the PREDICATE and so comes after the verb, as 'tired' in 'She was very tired' and 'mournful' in
'The music was very mournful'.

prefix see affix.

premodifier

A MODIFIER that comes before the main word of a NOUN PHRASE,
as 'green' in 'green dress' and 'pretty' in 'pretty houses'.

preposition

A word that relates two elements of a sentence, clause or
phrase together. Prepositions show how the elements relate
in time or space and generally precede the words that they
'govern'. Words governed by prepositions are nouns or pronouns. Prepositions are often very short words, as 'at', 'in',
'on', 'to', 'before' and 'after'. Some complex prepositions consist of two words, as 'ahead of', 'instead of', 'apart from', and
some consist of three, as 'with reference to', 'in accordance
with' and 'in addition to'. Examples of prepositions in sentences include 'The cat sat on the mat', 'We were at a concert',
'They are in shock', 'We are going to France', 'She arrived be-

fore me', 'Apart from you she has no friends' and 'We acted in accordance with your instructions'.

present continuous *see* **tense**.

present participle *see* **-ing words**.

present tense *see* **tense**.

principal clause *see* **main clause**.

progressive present *see* **tense**.

pronoun
A word that takes the place of a NOUN or a NOUN PHRASE. See PERSONAL PRONOUNS, HE, HER, HIM and HIS, RECIPROCAL PRONOUNS, REFLEXIVE PRONOUNS, DEMONSTRATIVE PRONOUNS, RELATIVE PRONOUNS, DISTRIBUTIVE PRONOUNS, INDEFINITE PRONOUNS and INTERROGATIVE PRONOUNS.

proper noun
A noun that refers to a particular individual or a specific thing. It is the 'name' of someone or something', as in Australia, Vesuvius, John Brown, River Thames, Rome and Atlantic Ocean. See CAPITAL LETTERS.

punctuation
The use of punctuation marks within a written text to enhance its meaning or fluency or to indicate aspects of pronunciation.

punctuation mark
One of the standardized symbols used in punctuation, as the FULL STOP, COLON, SEMICOLON, COMMA, QUESTION MARK, etc.

Q

question mark
The punctuation mark (?) that is placed at the end of a question or interrogative sentence, as in 'Who is he?', 'Where are they?', 'Why have they gone?', 'Whereabouts are they?', 'When are you going?' and 'What did he say?'. The question mark is sometimes known as the **query**.

question tag
A phrase that is interrogative in form but is not really asking a question. It is added to a statement to seek agreement, etc. Examples include 'That was a lovely meal, wasn't it?', 'You will be able to go, won't you?', 'He's not going to move house, is he?' and 'She doesn't drive, does she?' Sentences containing question tags have question marks at the end.

quotation marks or **inverted commas** or **quotes**
Punctuation marks that are used in DIRECT SPEECH. Quotation marks are also used to enclose titles of newspapers, books, plays, films, musical works and works of art, as in 'The Times', 'Animal Farm', 'Othello', 'My Fair Lady' and 'Portrait of the Artist'. Quotation marks may consist of a set of single inverted comas (' ') or a set of double inverted commas (" "). If a title, etc, is to be enclosed in quotation marks and the title is part

of a piece of writing already in quotation marks for some other reason, such as being part of direct speech, then the quotation marks round the title should be in the type of quotation marks opposite to the other ones. Thus, if the piece of writing is in single quotation marks then the title should be in double quotation marks. If the piece of prose is in double quotation marks the title should be in single quotation marks. Examples include 'Have you read "Wuthering Heights"?' and "Did you go to see 'My Fair Lady'?"

R

re-
A common prefix, meaning 'again', in verbs. In most cases it is not followed by a hyphen, as in 'to retrace one's footsteps', 'a retrial ordered by the judge' and 'reconsider his decision'. However, it should be followed by a hyphen if its absence is likely to lead to confusion with another word, as in 're-cover a chair'/'recover from an illness', 're-count the votes'/'recount a tale of woe', 'the re-creation of a 17th-century village for a film set'/'play tennis for recreation' and 're-form the group'/'reform the prison system'. In cases where the second element of a word begins with e, re- is traditionally followed by a hyphen, as in 're-educate', 're-entry' and 're-echo', but in modern usage the hyphen is frequently omitted.

reciprocal pronoun
A pronoun used to convey the idea of reciprocity or a two-way relationship. The reciprocal pronouns are 'each other' and 'one another'. Examples include 'They don't love each other any more', 'They seem to hate each other', 'We must try to help each other', 'The children were calling one another names', 'The two families were always criticizing one another' and 'The members of the family blame one another for their mother's death'.

reciprocal verb

A verb such as 'consult', 'embrace', 'marry', 'meet', etc, that expresses a mutual relationship, as in 'They met at the conference', 'She married him in June'.

reduplication

The process by which words are created by repetition or by semi-repetition. These include 'argy-bargy', 'dilly-dally', 'shilly-shally', 'flimflam', 'heebie-jeebies', 'hocus-pocus', 'hugger-mugger', 'knick-knack', and 'mish-mash'.

reflexive pronoun

A pronoun that ends in '-self' or '-selves' and refers back to a noun or pronoun that has occurred earlier in the same sentence. The reflexive pronouns include 'myself', 'ourselves'; 'yourself', 'yourselves'; 'himself', 'herself', 'itself', 'themselves'. Examples include 'The children washed themselves', 'He cut himself shaving', 'Have you hurt yourself?' and 'She has cured herself of the habit'.

Reflexive pronouns are sometimes used for emphasis, as in 'The town itself was not very interesting' and 'The headmaster himself punished the boys'. They can also be used to indicate that something has been done by somebody by his/her own efforts without any help, as in 'He built the house himself', 'We converted the attic ourselves'. They can also indicate that someone or something is alone, as in 'She lives by herself' and 'The house stands by itself'.

reflexive verb

A verb that has as its direct object a REFLEXIVE PRONOUN, e.g. 'They pride themselves on their skill as a team'.

regular sentence *see* **major sentence**.

regular verb *see* **irregular verb**.

relative clause
A SUBORDINATE CLAUSE that has the function of an adjective. It is introduced by a RELATIVE PRONOUN.

relative pronoun
A pronoun that introduces a RELATIVE CLAUSE. The relative pronouns are 'who', 'whom', 'whose', 'which' and 'that'. Examples of relative clauses introduced by relative pronouns include 'There is the man who stole the money', 'She is the person to whom I gave the money', 'This is the man whose wife won the prize', 'They criticized the work which he had done' and 'That's the house that I would like to buy'. Relative pronouns refer back to a NOUN or NOUN PHRASE in the MAIN CLAUSE. These nouns and noun phrases are known as ANTECEDENTS. The antecedents in the example sentences are respectively 'man', 'person', 'man', 'work' and 'house'.

   Sometimes the relative clause divides the parts of the main clause, as in 'The woman whose daughter is ill is very upset', 'The people whom we met on holiday were French' and 'The house that we liked best was too expensive'.

reported speech *see* **indirect speech**.

retro-
A prefix derived from Latin meaning 'back, backwards', as in retrograde, retrospect, retrorocket.

retronym
A word or phrase that has had to be renamed slightly in the

light of another invention, etc. For example, an ordinary guitar has become 'acoustic guitar' because of the existence of 'electric guitar'. Leather has sometimes become 'real leather' because of the existence of 'imitation leather'.

rhetorical question
A question that is asked to achieve some kind of effect and requires no answer. Examples include 'What's this country coming to?', 'Did you ever see the like', 'Why do these things happen to me?', 'Where did youth go?', 'Death, where is thy sting?' and 'Where does time go?'. See *also* INTERROGATIVE SENTENCE.

Roman type
The normal upright type used in printing, not BOLD or ITALIC type.

root means the same as **base**.

S

second person

The term used for the person or thing to whom one is talking. The term is applied to PERSONAL PRONOUNS. The second person singular whether acting as the subject of a sentence is 'you', as in 'I told you so', 'We informed you of our decision' and 'They might have asked you sooner'. The second person personal pronoun does not alter its form in the plural in English, unlike in some languages. The possessive form of the second person pronoun is 'yours' whether singular or plural, as in 'These books are not yours' and 'This pen must be yours'.

semicolon

A rather formal form of punctuation. It is mainly used between clauses that are not joined by any form of conjunction, as in 'We had a wonderful holiday; sadly they did not', 'She was my sister; she was also my best friend' and 'He was a marvellous friend; he is much missed'. A DASH is sometimes used instead of a semicolon but this more informal.

The semicolon is also used to form subsets in a long list or series of names so that the said list seems less complex, as in 'The young man who wants to be a journalist has applied everywhere. He has applied to *The Times* in London; *The Globe and Mail* in Toronto; *The Age* in Melbourne; *The Tribune* in Chicago'.

The semicolon is also sometimes used before 'however', 'nevertheless' 'hence', etc, as in 'We have extra seats for the concert; however you must not feel obliged to come'.

sentence
This is at the head of the hierarchy of grammar. All the other elements, such as words, phrases and clauses, go to make up sentences. It is difficult to define a sentence. In terms of recognizing a sentence visually it can be described as beginning with a capital letter and ending with a full stop, or with an equivalent to the full stop, such as an exclamation mark. It is a unit of grammar that can stand alone and make sense and obeys certain grammatical rules, such as usually having a SUBJECT and a PREDICATE, as in 'The girl banged the door', where 'the girl' is the subject and 'the door' is the predicate. See MAJOR SENTENCE, SIMPLE SENTENCE, COMPLEX SENTENCE.

set phrase see fixed phrase.

sexism
The domination of male values, which was formerly widespread in the English language whether this was intentional or not. Efforts are now being made to rectify this situation, although some of the suggestions made are rather extreme. Sensible progress has, however, been made. See HE; EACH; -MAN and -PERSON.

simile
A figure of speech in which something is compared with another and said to be like it. This is in contradistinction to META-

PHOR. where one thing is said actually to be another. Examples of similes include 'She is like an angel', 'Her hair is like silk', 'The old man's skin is like leather', He swims like a fish'.

simple sentence

A SENTENCE that cannot be broken down into other clauses. It generally contains a FINITE VERB. Simple sentences include 'The man stole the car', 'She nudged him' and 'He kicked the ball'. See COMPLEX SENTENCE and COMPOUND SENTENCE.

singular noun

A noun that refers to 'one' rather than 'more than one', which is the PLURAL form. See *also* IRREGULAR PLURAL.

spelling *see* **Appendix 1**.

split infinitive

An infinitive that has had another word in the form of an adverb placed between itself and 'to', as in 'to rudely push' and 'to quietly leave'. This was once considered a a great grammatical sin but the split infinitive is becoming acceptable in modern usage. In any case it sometimes makes for a clumsy sentence if one slavishly adheres to the correct form.

spoonerism

The accidental or deliberate transposition of the initial letters of two or more words, as in 'the queer old dean' instead of 'the dear old queen', 'a blushing crow' instead of a 'crushing blow' and 'a well-boiled icicle' instead of a 'well-oiled bicycle'. Spoonerisms are called after the Reverend William Archibald Spooner (1844-1930) of Oxford University.

stative present *see* **habitual** and **tense**.

stem see **base**.

strong verb
The more common term for IRREGULAR VERB.

structure word see **function word**.

subject
That which is spoken of in a sentence or clause and is usually either a NOUN, as in 'Birds fly' (birds is the noun as subject); a NOUN PHRASE, as in 'The people in the town dislike him' (the people in the town' is the subject); a PRONOUN, as in 'She hit the child' (she is the pronoun as subject); a PROPER NOUN, as in 'Paris is the capital of France'. See DUMMY SUBJECT.

subjunctive see **mood**.

subordinate clause
A clause that is dependent on another clause, namely the MAIN CLAUSE. Unlike the main clause, it cannot stand alone and make sense. Subordinate clauses are introduced by CONJUNCTIONS. Examples of conjunctions that introduce subordinate clauses include 'after', 'before', 'when', 'if', 'because' and 'since'. See ADVERBIAL CLAUSE; NOUN CLAUSE.

subordinating conjunction see **conjunction**.

suffix
An AFFIX that goes at the end of a word. The affix '-ness' is a suffix in 'softness' and 'prepreparedness'.

superlative form
The form of an adjective or adverb that expresses the highest or utmost degree of the quality or manner of the word. The

superlative forms follow the same rules as comparative forms except that they end in -*est* instead of -*er* and the longer ones use 'most' instead of 'more'. See *also* COMPARISON OF ADJECTIVES.

syllepsis is another word for **zeugma**.

synecdoche
A figure of speech in which the part is put for the whole. For example, in 'The power of the sceptre is fading', 'sceptre' is used for 'monarch'; in 'The country has a fleet of a hundred sail', 'sail' is used for 'ship'; In 'The actor had a very successful career on the boards', 'boards' is used for 'stage'.

T

tautology

Unnecessary repetition, as in 'new innovations', 'a see-through transparent material' and 'one after the other in succession'.

techno-

A prefix derived from Greek meaning 'craft, skill', as in technical, technology, technique, etc.

tele-

A prefix derived from Greek meaning 'distance', as in telephone, telescope and television, etc.

tense

The form of a verb that is used to show the time at which the action of the verb takes place. One of the tenses in English is the **present tense**. It is used to indicate an action now going on or a state now existing. A distinction can be made between the **habitual present**, which marks habitual or repeated actions or recurring events, and the **stative present**, which indicates something that is true at all times. Examples of habitual present include 'He works long hours' and 'She walks to work'. Examples of the stative tense include 'The world is round' and 'Everyone must die eventually'.

The **progressive present** or **continuous present** is

formed with the verb 'to be' and the present participle, as in, 'He is walking to the next village', 'She was driving along the road when she saw him' and 'They were worrying about the state of the economy'

The **past tense** refers to an action or state that has taken place before the present time. In the case of regular verbs it is formed by adding -*ed* to the base form of the verb, as in 'fear/ feared', 'look/looked', and 'turn/turned'. See *also* IRREGULAR VERBS.

The **future tense** refers to an action or state that will take place at some time in the future. It is formed with 'will' and 'shall'. Traditionally 'will' was used with the second and third person pronouns ('you', 'he/she/it', 'they') and 'shall' with the first person ('I' and 'we'), as in 'You will be bored', 'He will soon be home', 'They will leave tomorrow', 'I shall buy some bread' and 'We shall go by train'. Also traditionally 'shall' was used with the second and third persons to indicate emphasis, insistence, determination, refusal, etc, as in 'You shall go to the ball' and 'He shall not be admitted'. 'Will' was used with the first person in the same way, as in 'I will get even with him'.

In modern usage 'will' is generally used for the first person as well as for second and third, as in 'I will see you tomorrow' and 'We will be there soon' and 'shall' is used for emphasis, insistence, etc, for first, second and third persons.

The future tense can also be formed with the use of 'be about to' or 'be going to', as in 'We were about to leave' and 'They were going to look for a house.

Other tenses include the **perfect tense**, which is formed using the verb 'to have' and the past participle. In the case of regular verbs the past participle is formed by adding *ed* to the base form of the verb. See *also* IRREGULAR VERBS. Examples of the perfect tense include 'He has played his last match', 'We have travelled all day' and 'They have thought a lot about it'.

The **past perfect tense** or **pluperfect tense** is formed using the verb 'to have' and the past participle, as in 'She had no idea that he was dead' and 'They had felt unhappy about the situation'.

The **future perfect** is formed using the verb 'to have' and the past participle, as in 'He will have arrived by now'.

the

The definitive article, which usually refers back to something already identified or to something specific, as in 'Where is the key?', 'What have you done with the book that I gave you?' and 'We have found the book that had we lost'. It is also used to denote someone or something as being the only one, as in 'the House of Lords', 'the King of Spain' and 'the President of Russia' and to indicate a class or group, as in 'the aristocracy', 'the cat family' and 'the teaching profession'. The is sometimes pronounced 'thee' when it is used to identify someone or something unique or important, as in 'Is that the John Frame over there?' and 'She is the fashion designer of the moment'.

they see **he**.

third person

A third party, not the speaker or the person or thing being spoken to. Note that 'person' in this context can refer to things as well as people. 'Person' in this sense applies to personal pronouns. The third person singular forms are 'he', 'she' and 'it' when the subject of a sentence or clause, as in 'She will win' and 'It will be fine'. The third person singular forms are 'him', 'her', 'it' when the object, as in 'His behaviour hurt her' and 'She meant it'. The third person plural is 'they' when the subject, as in 'They have left' and 'They were angry' and 'them' when the object, as in 'His words made them angry' and 'We accompanied them'.

The possessive forms of the singular are 'his', 'hers' and 'its', as in 'he played his guitar' and 'The dog hurt its leg', and the the possessive form of the plural is theirs, as in 'That car is theirs' and 'They say that the book is theirs'. See HE.

to-infinitive

The INFINITIVE form of the verb when it is accompanied by 'to' rather than when it is the bare infinitive without 'to'. Examples of the to-infinitive include 'We were told to go', 'I didn't want to stay' and 'To get there on time we'll have to leave now'.

transitive verb

A verb that takes a DIRECT OBJECT. In the sentence 'The boy broke the window', 'window' is a direct object and so 'broke' (past tense of break) is a transitive verb. In the sentence 'She eats fruit', 'fruit' is a direct object and so 'eat' is a transitive verb. In the sentence 'They kill enemy soldiers' 'enemy soldiers' is a direct object and so 'kill' is a transitive verb. See IN-TRANSITIVE VERB.

U

ultra-
A prefix derived from Latin meaning 'beyond', as in ultraviolet and ultramodern.

umlaut
The SMALLCAPS DIACRITIC, which indicates a change of vowel sound in German, as in *mädchen*.

un-
A prefix with two meanings. It can mean either 'not', as in unclean, untrue and unwise. it can also mean 'back, reversal', as in undo, unfasten, unlatch and untie.

uncountable noun or **uncount noun**
A noun that is not usually pluralized or 'counted'. Such a noun is usually preceded by 'some', rather than 'a'. Uncountable nouns often refer to substances or commodities or qualities, processes and states. Examples of uncountable nouns include butter, china, luggage, petrol, sugar, heat, information, poverty, richness and warmth. In some situations it is possible to have a countable version of what is usually an uncountable noun. Thus 'sugar' is usually considered to be an uncountable noun but it can be used in a countable form in contexts such as 'I

take two sugars in my coffee please'. Some nouns exist in an uncountable and countable form. Examples include 'cake', as in 'Have some cake' and 'She ate three cakes' and 'She could not paint for lack of light' and 'the lights went out'.

uni-

A prefix derived from Latin meaning 'one', as in unicycle, unilateral and unity.

V

verb
The part of speech often known as a 'doing' word. Although this is rather restrictive, since it tends to preclude AUXILIARY VERBS, MODAL VERBS, etc, the verb is the word in a sentence that is most concerned with the action and is usually essential to the structure of the sentence. Verbs 'INFLECT' and indicate TENSE, voice, mood, number, number and person. Most of the information on verbs has been placed under related entries. See ACTIVE VOICE, AUXILIARY VERB, FINITE VERB, -ING FORMS, INTRANSITIVE VERB, IRREGULAR VERBS, LINKING VERB, MODAL VERB, MOOD, NON-FINITE VERB, PASSIVE VOICE and TRANSITIVE VERB.

verbal noun see gerund and -ing form.

verb phrase
A group of verb forms that have the same function as a single verb. Examples include 'have been raining', 'must have been lying', 'should not have been doing' and 'has been seen doing'.

virgule
A rare word for an oblique. See OBLIQUE.

vocative case
A case that is relevant mainly to languages such as Latin which are based on cases and inflections. In English the vocative is expressed by addressing someone, as 'John, could I see you for

a minute', or by some form of greeting, endearment or exclamation.

voice
One of the categories that describes verbs. It involves two ways of looking at the action of verbs. It is divided into ACTIVE VOICE and PASSIVE VOICE.

-ways

A suffix that to some extent acts as an alternative to -WISE in its first two meanings, as in lengthways.

weak verb

A less common term for a regular verb, in which inflection is effected by adding a letter or syllable (dawn, dawned) rather than a change of vowel (rise, rose). See IRREGULAR VERB.

who and whom

Who is the SUBJECT of a verb or clause, as in 'Who told you?' and 'the girls who took part in the play'. **Whom** is the OBJECT of a verb or preposition, as 'Whom did he tell?' and ' the people from whom he stole'.

whose and who's

These are liable to be confused because they sound the same. However they are not at all the same. **Who's** is a contraction of 'who is' and is used in speech and informal written contexts, as in 'Who's going to the cinema?' and 'Who's afraid of spiders'. **Whose** is a possessive pronoun or possessive adjective, as in 'That's the woman whose house was burgled' and 'Whose hat is this?'

-wise

A suffix with several meanings. It can mean 'indicating manner or way', as in clockwise. It can also mean 'in the position or direction of' as in lengthwise and breadthwise. It can also mean 'with reference to', as in careerwise. It can also mean 'clever, sensible', as in streetwise.

Z

zero plural
A plural form that has the same form as the singular. Examples include 'cod', 'deer', 'grouse' (game-bird) and 'sheep'. Some nouns have ordinary plurals and zero plurals as alternatives, as 'fish/fishes'. Nouns of measurement often have zero plurals, as in 'She is five foot three' and 'Six dozen eggs'.

zeugma or syllepsis
A figure of speech that uses a single word to apply to two words that are not appropriate to each other, as in 'We collected our coats and our baby', 'She left the building and her job' and 'She left in a taxi and a fit of hysterics'. Zeugma is similar to BATHOS.

Appendix 1

All of us have problem words that cause spelling difficulties but there are some words that are generally misspelt. These include:

A

abbreviation
abscess
absence
abysmal
accelerator
accessible
accessories
accommodate
accompaniment
accumulate
accurate
accustomed
achieve
aching
acknowledge
acknowledgement/
acknowledgment
acquaint
acquaintance
acquiesce

acquiescence
acquire
acquit
acquittal
acreage
across
actual
additional
address
adequate
adieu
adjacent
admissible
admittance
adolescence
adolescent
advantageous
advertisement
advice
advise
aerate

aerial
aesthetic
affect
affiliation
afforestation
aggravate
aggravation
aggregate
aggression
aggressive
aghast
agnosticism
agoraphobia
agreeable
agreed
aisle
alcohol
alfresco
alibis
align
alignment

allege
allergic
alleys
alligator
allocate
allotment
allotted
almond
alms
alphabetically
already
although
aluminium
ambiguous
amethyst
ammunition
anachronism
anaesthetic
analyse
analysis
anarchist
ancestor
ancestry
anemone
angrily
anguish
annihilate
annihilation
anniversary
announcement

annulled
annulment
anonymous
anorak
answered
Antarctic
antibiotic
antithesis
anxiety
apartheid
apologize
appalling
apparently
appearance
appendicitis
appreciate
approval
aquarium
aquiline
arbiter
arbitrary
arbitration
archaeology
architectural
Arctic
arguably
arrangement
arrival
artichoke
ascend

ascent
asphalt
asphyxiate
asphyxiation
assassin
assassinate
assessment
assistance
associate
asthma
asthmatic
astrakhan
atheist
atrocious
attach
attendant
attitude
aubergine
auburn
auctioneer
audible
aural
automatic
autumn
awful
awkward

B
bachelor
bagatelle

baggage
bailiff
ballast
ballerina
banana
banister
bankruptcy
banquet
barbecue
barometer
barrister
basically
basis
bassoon
battalion
bazaar
beautiful
befriend
beguile
behaviour
beleaguer
belief
believe
belligerent
benefited
bequeath
berserk
besiege
bettered
bevelled

bewitch
bias
bicycle
biennial
bigamous
bigoted
bilingual
biscuit
bivouacked
blancmange
blasphemous
blasphemy
bleary
blitz
bodily
bonfire
bootee
borough
bouquet
bourgeois
boutique
bracketed
braille
brassiere
breadth
breathalyser
brief
broccoli
brochure
bronchitis

bruise
brusque
buccaneer
Buddhist
budding
budgerigar
budgeted
buffeted
bulletin
bumptious
bungalow
buoyancy
buoyant
bureau
bureaucracy
business
buttoned

C

cabbage
cafeteria
caffeine
camouflage
campaign
campaigned
cancelled
cancerous
candour
cannabis
cannibal

canvassing
capability
capillary
capitalist
caravan
carbohydrate
carburettor
career
caress
caries
carriage
cartoonist
cashier
cassette
castanets
casualty
catalogue
catarrh
catechism
catering
cauliflower
cautious
ceiling
cellophane
cemetery
centenary
centilitre
centimetre
certainty
champagne

championed
chancellor
changeable
channelled
characteristic
chasm
chauffeur
cheetah
cherish
chief
chilblain
chintz
chiropody
chisel
choreographer
choreography
chronically
chrysanthemum
cigarette
cinnamon
circuitous
cistern
civilian
claustrophobia
clientele
clique
coalesce
cocoa
coconut
coffee

cognac
coincidence
colander
collaborate
collapsible
colleague
colonel
colossal
comically
commandeer
commemorate
commentator
commercial
commiserate
commission
commissionaire
commitment
committal
committed
committee
communicate
commuter
companion
comparative
comparison
compatibility
compelled
competitive
computer
conceal

concealment
conceit
conceive
concession
concurrent
concussion
condemned
condescend
confectionery
conference
confetti
congeal
congratulations
conjunctivitis
conned
connoisseur
conscience
conscientious
conscious
consequently
consignment
consolation
conspicuous
constitute
consumer
contemptible
continent
continuous
contraception
contradictory

controlled
controller
controversial
convalesce
convenient
convertible
conveyed
convolvulus
coolly
cooperate
cooperative
coordinate
copying
coquette
corduroy
co-respondent
coronary
correspondence
correspondent
corridor
corroborate
corrugated
cosmopolitan
cosseted
councillor
counselling
counterfeit
courageous
courteous
crèche

credible
credited
crematorium
creosote
crescent
crisis
criterion
crocheted
crocodile
croupier
crucial
crucifixion
cruelly
cruise
cryptic
cubicle
cupful
curable
curiosity
curious
currency
curriculum vitae
customary
cynic
cynicism
cynosure

D

dachshund
daffodil

dahlia	demonstrate	dilemma
dais	denouement	dilettante
damage	denunciation	diminish
dandruff	dependence	diminution
darkened	depth	dinosaur
debatable	derailment	diphtheria
debauched	dermatitis	diphthong
debility	derogatory	disadvantageous
deceased	descend	disagreeable
deceit	descendant	disagreed
deceive	desiccate	disagreement
deciduous	desperate	disappearance
decipher	detach	disappeared
decoyed	detachable	disappoint
decrease	detergent	disapproval
decreed	deterred	disastrous
defamatory	deterrent	disbelief
defeat	deuce	disbelieve
defendant	develop	discipline
defied	developed	discotheque
definite	development	discouraging
definitely	diabetes	discourteous
dehydrate	diagnosis	discrepancy
deign	dialogue	discrimination
deliberate	diametrically	discussion
delicatessen	diaphragm	disease
delicious	diarrhoea	disguise
delinquent	difference	dishevelled
delirious	different	dishonourable
demeanour	dilapidated	disillusion

disinfectant
disinherited
dismissal
disobeyed
disparage
dispelled
disposal
dispossess
dissatisfaction
dissatisfy
dissect
disseminate
dissent
dissimilar
dissipated
dissipation
dissociate
dissolute
dissuade
distilled
distillery
distinguish
distraught
disuse
divisible
documentary
doggerel
domineering
donate
doubt

dragooned
drastically
draughty
drooled
drooped
drunkenness
dubious
dumbfounded
dungarees
duress
dutiful
dynamite
dysentery
dyspepsia

E

eccentric
ecclesiastic
ecologically
economically
ecstasy
eczema
effective
effervescence
efficacious
efficient
effrontery
eightieth
elaborate
electrician

elevenses
eligible
emancipate
embarrass
embarrassment
emergence
emergent
emolument
emotional
emphasize
employee
emptied
enable
encourage
encyclopedia
endeavour
endurance
energetically
enervate
engineer
enough
ensuing
entailed
enthusiasm
enumerate
epilepsy
equalize
equalled
equipped
erroneous

erudite
escalator
escapism
espionage
essence
essential
estranged
etiquette
euthanasia
eventually
evidently
exaggerate
exaggeration
exalt
exasperate
exceed
exceedingly
excellent
excessive
exchequer
excommunicate
exercise
exhaust
exhibit
exhilarate
exorcise
explanation
exquisite
extinguish
extraneous

extravagant

F
fabulous
facetious
faeces
Fahrenheit
fallacious
fanatic
farcical
fascinate
fatigue
fatuous
February
feeler
feign
ferocious
festooned
feud
feudal
fevered
fiasco
fibre
fictitious
fiend
fierce
fiery
filial
finesse
flabbergasted

flaccid
flammable
flannelette
fluent
fluoridate
fluoride
fluoridize
foliage
forcible
foreigner
forfeit
forthwith
fortieth
fortuitous
fortunately
frailty
frankincense
fraudulent
freedom
freight
frequency
friend
frolicked
fuchsia
fugitive
fulfil
fulfilled
fulfilment
fullness
fulsome

furious
furniture
furthered

G
gaiety
galloped
garrison
garrotted
gases
gateau
gauge
gazetteer
geisha
generator
genuine
gerbil
gesticulate
ghastly
ghetto
gigantic
gingham
giraffe
glamorous
glamour
glimpse
global
gluttonous
glycerine
gnarled

gnash
goitre
gossiped
government
graffiti
grammar
grandeur
gratefully
gratitude
gratuitous
greetings
gregarious
grief
grieve
grovelled
gruesome
guarantee
guarantor
guard
guardian
guest
guillotine
guinea
guise
guitar
gymkhana
gypsy/gipsy

H
haemoglobin

haemorrhage
halcyon
hallucination
hammered
handfuls
handicapped
handkerchief
happened
harangue
harass
harlequin
haughty
hazard
hearse
height
heightened
heinous
heir
herbaceous
hereditary
heroism
hesitate
hiccup, hiccough
hideous
hierarchy
hieroglyphics
hijack
hilarious
hindrance
hippopotamus

holiday
holocaust
homonym
honorary
honour
hooligan
horoscope
horrible
horticulture
hullabaloo
humorous
humour
hurricane
hurried
hygiene
hyphen
hypnosis
hypochondria
hypocrisy
hypotenuse
hypothesis
hypothetical
hysterical

I

icicle
ideological
idiosyncrasy
ignorance
illegible

illegitimate
illiberal
illiterate
imaginative
imitation
immaculate
immediate
immemorial
immoral
immovable
impasse
impeccable
imperative
imperceptible
imperious
impetuous
implacable
impresario
imprisoned
imprisonment
inaccessible
inadmissible
inappropriate
inaugural
incandescent
incessant
incipient
incognito
incommunicado
inconceivable

incongruous
incontrovertible
incorrigible
incredulous
incriminate
incubator
incurred
indefatigable
indefinable
indefinite
independence
independent
indescribable
indict
indictment
indigenous
indigestible
indomitable
indubitable
ineligible
inescapable
inexcusable
inexhaustible
infallible
infatuated
inferred
infinitive
inflamed
inflammable
inflationary

ingratiate
ingredient
inhabitant
inheritance
inhibition
iniquitous
initiate
initiative
innate
innocuous
innumerable
innumerate
inoculate
insecticide
inseparable
insincere
insistence
instalment
instantaneous
intercept
interference
interior
intermediate
intermittent
interpret
interpretation
interrogate
interrupt
interview
intrigue

intrinsically
intuition
intuitive
invariably
inveigle
inveterate
involuntary
involvement
irascible
irrelevant
irreparable
irreplaceable
irresistible
irresponsible
irrevocable
irritable
italicize
itinerant
itinerary

J

jackal
Jacuzzi
jeopardize
jettisoned
jewellery
jodhpurs
juggernaut
jugular

K

kaleidoscopic
karate
keenness
khaki
kidnapped
kilometre
kiosk
kitchenette
kleptomania
knick-knack
knowledgeable
kowtow

L

labelled
laboratory
labyrinth
lackadaisical
laddered
lager
language
languor
languorous
laryngitis
larynx
lassitude
latitude
laundered
launderette

layette
league
leanness
ledger
legendary
legible
legitimate
length
lengthened
leukaemia
levelled
liaise
liaison
lieu
lieutenant
lilac
limousine
lineage
linen
lingerie
linguist
liqueur
literature
litre
livelihood
loneliness
loosened
loquacious
lorgnette
lucrative

lucre
luggage
lugubrious
luminous
luscious
lustre
luxurious
lyric

M

macabre
maelstrom
magician
magnanimous
mahogany
maintenance
malaise
malaria
malignant
manageable
management
mannequin
manoeuvre
mantelpiece
manually
margarine
marijuana
marquee
martyr
marvellous

marzipan
masochist
massacre
matinee
mayonnaise
meagre
measurement
medallion
medieval
mediocre
melancholy
meningitis
meringue
messenger
meteorological
metropolitan
microphone
midday
migraine
mileage
milieu
millionaire
mimicked
mimicry
miniature
miraculous
mirrored
miscellaneous
mischief
mischievous

misogynist
misshapen
misspell
misspent
modelled
modelling
morgue
mortgage
mosquito
mountaineer
moustache
multitudinous
muscle
museum
mysterious
mythical

N

naive
narrative
naughty
nausea
nautical
necessary
necessity
negligence
negligible
negotiate
neighbourhood
neither

neurotic
neutral
niche
niece
ninetieth
ninth
nocturnal
nonentity
notably
noticeably
notoriety
nuance
numbered
numerate
numerous
nutrient
nutritious

O

obedient
obese
obituary
oblige
oblique
oblivious
obnoxious
obscene
obscenity
obsessive
obstetrician

occasion
occupancy
occupier
occupying
occurred
occurrence
octogenarian
odorous
odour
offence
offered
official
officious
ominous
omission
omitted
oneself
opaque
ophthalmic
opinion
opponent
opportunity
opposite
orchestra
ordinary
original
orthodox
orthopaedic
oscillate
ostracize

outlying
outrageous
overdraft
overrate
overreach
overwrought
oxygen

P

pacifist
pageant
pamphlet
panacea
panegyric
panicked
papered
parachute
paraffin
paragraph
paralyse
paralysis
paraphernalia
parcelled
parliament
paroxysm
parquet
partially
participant
particle
partner

passenger
passers-by
pastime
patterned
pavilion
peaceable
peculiar
pejorative
pencilled
penicillin
peppered
perceive
perennial
perilous
permissible
permitted
pernicious
perpetrate
persistence
personnel
persuasion
perusal
pessimism
pessimistically
pesticide
phantom
pharmacy
pharyngitis
pharynx
phenomenon

phial
phlegm
physician
physiotherapist
picketed
picnic
picnicked
picturesque
pioneered
pious
piteous
pitiful
plaintiff
plausible
pleurisy
pneumonia
poignant
politician
pollution
polythene
porridge
portrait
portray
positive
possession
possibility
posthumous
potatoes
precede
precedent

precinct
precipice
precocious
preference
preferred
prejudice
preliminary
prepossessing
prerequisite
prerogative
prescription
presence
preservative
prestige
prestigious
pretentious
prevalent
priest
primitive
procedure
proceed
procession
professional
profiteering
prohibit
promiscuous
pronunciation
propeller
proposal
proprietor

prosecute
protagonist
protein
provocation
prowess
psalm
psyche
psychiatric
psychic
publicly
pursuit
putative
pyjamas

Q

quarrelsome
questionnaire
queue
quintet

R

rabies
radioed
radios
railing
rancour
ransack
rapturous
reassurance
rebelled

rebellious
recalcitrant
receipt
receive
recommend
reconnaissance
reconnoitre
recruitment
recurrence
redundant
referee
reference
referred
regatta
regrettable
regretted
rehabilitation
reign
relevant
relief
relieve
reminisce
reminiscence
remuneration
rendezvous
repertoire
repetitive
reprieve
reprisal
requisite

rescind
resemblance
reservoir
resistance
resourceful
responsibility
restaurant
restaurateur
resurrection
resuscitate
retrieve
reunion
reveille
revelry
revenue
reversible
rhapsody
rheumatism
rhododendron
rhomboid
rhubarb
rhyme
rhythm
ricochet
righteous
rigorous
rigour
risotto
riveted
rogue

roughage
roulette
royalty
rucksack
ruinous
rummage
rumour

S

sabotage
sacrilege
saddened
salmon
salvage
sanctuary
sandwich
sanitary
sapphire
satellite
scaffolding
scandalous
scenic
sceptre
schedule
scheme
schizophrenic
schooner
sciatica
science
scissors

scruple
scrupulous
scurrilous
scythe
secretarial
secretary
sedative
sedentary
sensitive
separate
sergeant
serrated
serviceable
serviette
settee
shampooed
shattered
sheikh
sheriff
shield
shovelled
shuddered
siege
significant
silhouette
simply
simultaneous
sincerely
sixtieth
skeleton

skilful
slanderous
slaughter
sleigh
sleight of hand
sluice
smattering
smithereens
snivelled
soccer
solemn
solicitor
soliloquy
soloist
sombre
somersault
sophisticated
sovereign
spaghetti
spectre
spherical
sphinx
sponsor
spontaneity
spontaneous
squabble
squandered
squawk
staccato
staggered

stammered
statistics
statutory
stealth
stereophonic
stirrup
storage
strait-laced
straitjacket
strategic
strength
strenuous
stupor
suave
subpoena
subtle
succeed
successful
successor
succinct
succulent
succumb
suddenness
suede
sufficient
suffocate
suicide
sullenness
summoned
supercilious

superfluous
supersede
supervise
supervisor
supplementary
surgeon
surveillance
surveyor
susceptible
suspicious
sweetener
sycamore
symmetry
sympathize
symphony
synagogue
syndicate
synonym
syringe

T
tableau
taciturn
taffeta
tangerine
tangible
tattoo
technique
teenager
televise

temperature
tenuous
terrifically
terrifying
territory
terrorist
therapeutic
therefore
thief
thinness
thirtieth
thorough
thoroughfare
threshold
thrombosis
throughout
thwart
thyme
tightened
titivate
tobacconist
toboggan
toffee
tomatoes
tomorrow
tonsillitis
topsy turvy
tornadoes
torpedoes
torpor

tortoiseshell
tortuous
totalled
tourniquet
towelling
trafficked
tragedy
traitorous
tranquillity
tranquillizer
transcend
transferable
transferred
transparent
travelled
traveller
tremor
troublesome
trousseau
truism
trustee
tsetse
tuberculosis
tumour
tunnelled
tureen
turquoise
twelfth
typhoon
tyranny

U

unanimous
unconscious
undoubted
unduly
unequalled
unique
unnecessary
unremitting
unrequited
unrivalled
upheaval
uproarious

V

vaccinate
vacuum
vague
vanilla
variegate
vehement
vendetta
veneer
ventilator
verandah
vermilion
veterinary
vetoes
vice versa
vicissitude

vigorous
vigour
viscount
visibility
vivacious
vociferous
voluminous
volunteered
vulnerable

W
walkie-talkie
walloped
warrior
wastage
watered
weakened

wearisome
Wednesday
weight
weird
whereabouts
wherewithal
widened
width
wield
wintry
witticism
wizened
woebegone
wooden
woollen
worsened
worship

worshipped
wrapper
wrath
wreak
writhe

X
xylophone

Y
yield
yoghurt

Z
zealous
zigzagged

Appendix 2

Some words with totally different meanings have similar spellings and therefore can be easily confused.

Some examples are:

aboard	abroad	allusion	delusion
accept	except		illusion
access	excess	altar	alter
acme	acne	alteration	altercation
ad	add	alternately	alternatively
adapter	adaptor	amateur	amateurish
addition	edition	amend	emend
adverse	averse	amiable	amicable
advice	advise	among	between
aesthetic	ascetic	amoral	immoral
affect	effect		immortal
affluent	effluent	angel	angle
ail	ale	annals	annuals
air	heir	annex	annexe
all	awl	annuals	annals
allay	alley	antiquated	antique
allegory	allergy	arc	ark
alley	allay	arisen	arose
alliterate	illiterate	artist	artiste
allude	elude	ascent	assent

ascetic	aesthetic	bean	been
assay	essay		being
assent	ascent	beat	beet
astrology	astronomy	beau	bow
ate	eaten	became	become
aural	oral	beech	beach
averse	adverse	been	bean
awl	all		being
axes	axis	beer	bier
bad	bade	beet	beat
bade	bid	befallen	befell
bail	bale	began	begun
	bale out	being	bean
baited	bated		been
ball	bawl	belief	believe
ballet	ballot	bell	belle
banns	bans	bellow	below
bare	bear	beret	berry
barn	baron		bury
	barren	berth	birth
base	bass	beside	besides
bated	baited	between	among
bath	bathe	bid	bade
baton	batten	bier	beer
bawl	ball	bight	bite
bazaar	bizarre	birth	berth
beach	beech	bit	bitten

bite	bight	bow	beau
bizarre	bazaar	bow	bough
blew	blown	boy	buoy
blew	blue	brae	bray
bloc	block	brake	break
blond	blonde	brassière	brazier
blow	blown	bray	brae
	blew	brazier	brassière
blue	blew	breach	breech
boar	boor	bread	bred
	bore	break	brake
board	bored	breath	breathe
boast	boost	bred	bread
bonny	bony	breech	breach
bookie	bouquet	bridal	bridle
boor	boar	broach	brooch
	bore	broke	broken
boost	boast	brooch	broach
bootee	booty	buffet [buffit]	buffet [boofa]
bore	boar	buoy	boy
	boor	burgh	borough
bore	born	bury	beret
	borne		berry
borough	burgh	but	butt
bough	bow	buy	by
bound	bounded		bye
bouquet	bookie	cache	cash

caddie	caddy
calf	calve
callous	callus
calve	calf
came	come
canned	could
cannon	canon
can't	cant
canvas	canvass
carat	carrot
cart	kart
cartilage	cartridge
carton	cartoon
cartridge	cartilage
cash	cache
cast	caste
cavalier	cavalry
ceiling	sealing
cell	sell
cellular	cellulose
censor	censure
cent	scent
	sent
centenarian	centenary
cereal	serial
chafe	chaff
charted	chartered

chased	chaste
cheap	cheep
check	cheque
checkered	chequered
cheep	cheap
cheque	check
chilli	chilly
choir	quire
choose	chose
	chosen
chord	cord
chose	choose
	chosen
chute	shoot
cite	sight
	site
clothes	cloths
coarse	course
collage	college
coma	comma
come	came
comma	coma
commissionaire	commissioner
complement	compliment
complementary	complimentary
concert	consort

confidant	confidante	crevasse	crevice
	confident	crochet	crotchet
conscience	conscientious	cue	queue
	conscious	curb	kerb
consort	concert	currant	current
consul	council	curtsy	courtesy
	counsel	cygnet	signet
continual	continuous	cymbal	symbol
coop	coup	dairy	diary
coral	corral	dam	damn
cord	chord	dammed	damned
co-respondent	correspondent	damn	dam
cornet	coronet	dear	deer
cornflour	cornflower	decry	descry
coronet	cornet	deer	dear
corps	corpse	delusion	allusion
corral	coral		illusion
correspondent	co-respondent	dependant	dependent
cost	costed	deprecate	depreciate
could	canned	descendant	descendent
council	counsel	descry	decry
	consul	desert	dessert
councillor	counsellor	device	devise
coup	coop	devolution	evolution
course	coarse	dew	due
courtesy	curtsy		Jew
creak	creek	diary	dairy

did	done	dye	die
die	dye	dyed	died
died	dyed	dyeing	dying
dinghy	dingy	earthly	earthy
disbelief	disbelieve	easterly	eastern
discus	discuss	eaten	ate
doe	dough	eclipse	ellipse
doily	dolly	economic	economical
done	did	edition	addition
dough	doe	eerie	eyrie
draft	draught	effect	affect
dragon	dragoon	effluent	affluent
draught	draft	elder	eldest
drawn	drew	elicit	illicit
drank	drunk	eligible	legible
drew	drawn	ellipse	eclipse
driven	drove	elude	allude
drunk	drank	emend	amend
dual	duel	emigrant	immigrant
ducks	dux	emigration	immigration
dudgeon	dungeon	emission	omission
due	dew	emphasis	emphasize
	Jew	employee	employer
duel	dual	ensure	insure
dully	duly	entomologist	etymologist
dungeon	dudgeon	envelop	envelope
dux	ducks		

epigram	epitaph	fair	fare
	epithet	fairy	faerie
ere	err	fallen	fell
erotic	erratic		felled
err	ere	fare	fair
erratic	erotic	fate	fête
escapement	escarpment	faun	fawn
essay	assay	feat	feet
etymologist	entomologist	feign	fain
evolution	devolution	feint	faint
ewe	yew	fell	fallen
	you		felled
except	accept	ferment	foment
excess	access	fête	fate
executioner	executor	fiancé	fiancée
exercise	exorcise	filed	filled
expand	expend	final	finale
expansive	expensive	fir	fur
expatiate	expiate	fission	fissure
expend	expand	flair	flare
expensive	expansive	flammable	inflammable
expiate	expatiate	flare	flair
extant	extinct	flea	flee
eyrie	eerie	flew	flu
faerie	fairy		flue
fain	feign	flew	flown
faint	feint	flocks	phlox

floe	flow	forward	foreword
flour	flower	forwent	forgone
floury	flowery	foul	fowl
flow	floe	found	founded
flower	flour	fount	font
flowery	floury	four	fore
flown	flew	fourth	forth
flu	flew	fowl	foul
	flue	franc	frank
foment	ferment	freeze	frieze
font	fount	froze	frozen
forbade	forbidden	funeral	funereal
fore	four	fur	fir
foregone	forgone	gabble	gable
foresaw	foreseen	gaff	gaffe
foreword	forward	gait	gate
forgave	forgiven	galleon	gallon
forgone	foregone	gamble	gambol
forgone	forwent	gaol	goal
forgot	forgotten	gate	gait
forsaken	forsook	gave	given
forswore	forsworn	genie	genius
fort	forte	genus	
	forty	genteel	gentile
forth	fourth		gentle
forty	fort	genus	genie
	forte		genius

gild	guild	halve	half
gilt	guilt	hangar	hanger
given	gave	hanged	hung
glacier	glazier	hanger	hangar
goal	gaol	hare	hair
gone	went	hart	heart
gorilla	guerrilla	heal	heel
gourmand	gourmet	hear	here
gradation	graduation	heart	hart
grate	great	heel	heal
grew	grown	heir	air
grief	grieve	here	hear
grill	grille	heron	herring
griped	gripped	hew	hue
grisly	gristly	hewed	hewn
	grizzly	hid	hidden
grope	group	higher	hire
ground	grounded	him	hymn
grown	grew	hire	higher
guerrilla	gorilla	hoar	whore
guild	gild	hoard	horde
guilt	gilt	hoarse	horse
hail	hale	hole	whole
hair	hare	honorary	honourable
half	halve	hoop	whoop
hallo	hallow	hoped	hopped
	halo	horde	hoard

horse	hoarse	inhuman	inhumane
hue	hew	insure	ensure
human	humane	intelligent	intelligible
humiliation	humility	interment	internment
hung	hanged	invertebrate	inveterate
hymn	him	jam	jamb
idle	idol	Jew	dew
illegible	ineligible		due
illicit	elicit	jib	jibe
illiterate	alliterate	judicial	judicious
illusion	allusion	junction	juncture
	delusion	kart	cart
immigrant	emigrant	kerb	curb
immigration	emigration	key	quay
immoral	amoral	knave	nave
	immortal	knead	kneed
immorality	immortality		need
impetuous	impetus	knew	known
impracticable	impractical	knew	new
inapt	inept	knight	night
incredible	incredulous	knightly	nightly
indigenous	indigent	knit	nit
industrial	industrious	knot	not
ineligible	illegible	knotty	naughty
inept	inapt	know	no
inflammable	flammable	known	knew
ingenious	ingenuous	lade	laid

lay	lied	liqueur	liquor
lain	lane	literal	literary
lair	layer		literate
lama	llama	llama	lama
lane	lain	load	lode
laterally	latterly	loan	lone
lath	lathe	loath	loathe
latterly	laterally	local	locale
lay	lied	lode	load
layer	lair	lone	loan
lea	lee	looped	loped
lead	led		lopped
leak	leek	loose	lose
led	lead	loot	lute
lee	lea	loped	lopped
leek	leak		looped
legible	eligible	lose	loose
lemming	lemon	loth	loathe
leopard	leper	lumbar	lumber
lessen	lesson	lute	loot
liable	libel	lyre	liar
liar	lyre	macaroni	macaroon
libel	liable	made	maid
licence	license	magnate	magnet
lied	lay	maid	made
lightening	lightning	mail	male
lineament	liniment	main	mane

maize	maze	mettle	metal
male	mail	mews	muse
mane	main	mien	mean
maniac	manic	might	mite
manner	manor	miner	minor
mare	mayor	minister	minster
marina	merino	missal	missile
marshal	martial	mistaken	mistook
marten	martin	mite	might
martial	marshal	moat	mote
martin	marten	modal	model
mask	masque		module
mat	matt	momentary	momentous
mayor	mare		momentum
maze	maize	moose	mouse
mean	mien		mousse
meat	meet	moped	mo-ped
	mete out		mopped
medal	meddle	moral	morale
mediate	meditate	morality	mortality
meet	meat	mote	moat
	mete out	motif	motive
merino	marina	mouse	moose
metal	mettle		mousse
mete out	meat	mucous	mucus
	meet	multiple	multiply
meter	metre	muscle	mussel

muse	mews	oar	ore
mussel	muscle	of	off
mystic	mystique	official	officious
naught	nought	omission	emission
naughty	knotty	oral	aural
naval	navel	ore	oar
nave	knave	organism	orgasm
navel	naval	outdid	outdone
navvy	navy	overcame	overcome
nay	née	overdid	overdone
	neigh	overran	overrun
need	knead	overtaken	overtook
	kneed	overthrew	overthrown
negligent	negligible	packed	pact
neigh	nay	pail	pale
	née	pain	pane
net	nett	pair	pare
new	knew		pear
night	knight	palate	palette
nightly	knightly		pallet
nit	knit	pale	pail
no	know	palette	palate
northerly	northern		pallet
not	knot	pane	pain
nougat	nugget	par	parr
nought	naught	pare	pear
nugget	nougat		pair

parr	par	piece	peace
passed	past	pier	peer
pastel	pastille	pined	pinned
pate	pâté	piped	pipped
	patty	pique	peak
peace	piece		peek
peak	peek	pistil	pistol
	pique	pizza	piazza
peal	peel	place	plaice
pear	pair	plain	plane
	pare	plaintiff	plaintive
pearl	purl	plait	plate
peasant	pheasant	plane	plain
pedal	peddle	plate	plait
peek	peak	plum	plumb
	pique	politic	political
peel	peal	pool	pull
peer	pier	poplar	popular
pence	pennies	pore	pour
pendant	pendent	pored	poured
pennies	pence	poser	poseur
perquisite	prerequisite	pour	pore
personal	personnel	poured	pored
petrel	petrol	practicable	practical
pheasant	peasant	practice	practise
phlox	flocks	pray	prey
piazza	pizza	precede	proceed

premier	première	quiet	quite
prerequisite	perquisite	quire	choir
prey	pray	quite	quiet
price	prise	racket	racquet
	prize	radar	raider
principal	principle	raged	ragged
prise	price	raider	radar
	prize	rain	reign
private	privet		rein
prize	prise	raise	raze
	price	rampant	rampart
proceed	precede	ran	run
profit	prophet	rang	ringed
program	programme		rung
proof	prove	rap	wrap
property	propriety	raped	rapped
prophecy	prophesy	rapped	rapt
prophet	profit		wrapped
propriety	property	rated	ratted
prostate	prostrate	raze	raise
prove	proof	read	red
pull	pool	read	reed
purl	pearl	real	reel
put	putt	red	read
quash	squash	reel	real
quay	key	refuge	refugee
queue	cue	regal	regale

reign	rain	rout	route
	rein	row	roe
relief	relieve	rowed	road
reproof	reprove		rode
respectful	respective	ruff	rough
rest	wrest	run	ran
retch	wretch	rung	wrung
review	revue	rye	wry
rhyme	rime	sail	sale
ridden	rode	salon	saloon
right	rite	sang	sung
	write	sank	sunk
rime	rhyme		sunken
ring	wring	saviour	savour
ringed	rang	saw	seen
	rung	sawed	sawn
		scared	scarred
risen	rose	scene	seen
rite	right	scent	cent
	write		sent
road	rode	sceptic	septic
	rowed	scraped	scrapped
rode	ridden	sculptor	sculpture
roe	row	sea	see
rôle	roll	sealing	ceiling
rose	risen	seam	seem
rote	wrote	sear	seer
rough	ruff		sere

secret	secrete	shelf	shelve
see	sea	shoe	shoo
seem	seam	shook	shaken
seen	saw	shoot	chute
seen	scene	shorn	sheared
seer	sear		sheered
	sere	showed	shown
sell	cell	shrank	shrunk
sensual	sensuous	sight	cite
sent	scent		site
	scent	signet	cygnet
septic	sceptic	silicon	silicone
sere	sear	singeing	singing
	seer	sinuous	sinus
serial	cereal	site	cite
series	serious		sight
sew	so	skies	skis
	sow	slain	slew
sewed	sewn	slated	slatted
sewer	sower	slay	sleigh
sewn	sewed	slew	slain
sewn	sown	sloe	slow
sextant	sexton	sloped	slopped
shaken	shook	slow	sloe
shear	sheer	smelled	smelt
sheared	sheered	sniped	snipped
	shorn	so	sew
			sow

soar	sore	stank	stunk
sociable	social	stare	stair
solder	soldier	stared	starred
sole	soul	stationary	stationery
some	sum	statue	statute
son	sun	staunch	stanch
soot	suit	stayed	staid
sore	soar	steak	stake
soul	sole	steal	steel
southerly	southern	step	steppe
sow	sew	stile	style
	so	stimulant	stimulus
sowed	sown	stock	stalk
sower	sewer	stocked	stoked
sown	sewn	storey	story
spared	sparred	straight	strait
speciality	specialty	straightened	straitened
species	specious	stratum	stratus
sped	speeded	strewed	strewn
spoke	spoken	strife	strive
sprang	sprung	striped	stripped
squash	quash	strive	strife
staid	stayed	striven	strove
stair	stare	stunk	stank
stake	steak	sty	stye
stalk	stock	style	stile
stanch	staunch	suede	swede

suit	soot	tare	tear
suite	sweet	taught	taut
sum	some	tax	tacks
summary	summery	tea	tee
sun	son	team	teem
sundae	Sunday	tear	tare
sung	sang	tear	tier
sunk	sank	tee	tea
	sunken	teem	team
super	supper	teeth	teethe
surplice	surplus	temporal	temporary
swam	swum	tendon	tenon
swede	suede	tenor	tenure
sweet	suite	testimonial	testimony
swelled	swollen	their	there
swingeing	swinging		they're
swollen	swelled	thorough	through
swore	sworn	thrash	thresh
swum	swam	threw	through
symbol	cymbal	threw	thrown
tacks	tax	throes	throws
tail	tale	throne	thrown
taken	took	through	thorough
tale	tail	through	threw
taped	tapped	thrown	throne
taper	tapir	throws	throes
tapped	taped	thyme	time

tic	tick	tycoon	typhoon
tier	tear	tyre	tire
tiled	tilled	unaware	unawares
timber	timbre	unconscionable	unconscious
time	thyme	undid	undone
tire	tyre	unwanted	unwonted
to	too	urban	urbane
	two	vacation	vocation
toe	tow	vain	vane
tomb	tome		vein
ton	tonne	vale	veil
	tun	venal	venial
too	to	veracity	voracity
	two	vertex	vortex
took	taken	vigilant	vigilante
topi	toupee	vocation	vacation
tore	torn	voracity	veracity
tow	toe	vortex	vertex
trait	tray	wafer	waver
treaties	treatise	waged	wagged
trod	trodden	waif	waive
troop	troupe		wave
tun	ton	waist	waste
	tonne	want	wont
turban	turbine	warden	warder
two	to	ware	wear
	too	waste	waist

wave	waif	wore	worn
	waive	would	willed
waver	wafer	would	wood
way	weigh		wooed
weak	week		
wear	ware	wove	woven
weekly	weakly	wrap	rap
weigh	way	wrapped	rapped
went	gone		rapt
westerly	western	wreak	wreck
wet	whet	wreath	wreathe
whit	wit	wrest	rest
whole	hole	wretch	retch
whoop	hoop	wring	ring
whore	hoar	write	right
willed	would		rite
winded	wound	wrote	rote
wit	whit	wrote	written
withdrawn	withdrew	wrung	rung
wittily	wittingly	wry	rye
woe	woo	yew	ewe
woke	woken		you
wont	want	yoke	yolk
woo	woe	yore	your